Advance Praise

Your Veterinary Dream Team is the roadmap that veterinary practices have been missing. Gwendolyn Delavar demystifies recruiting at the practice level, from building an in-house pipeline to knowing when to partner with an external recruiter. She blends ethics with practicality, tackling sensitive topics like poaching and contracts with clarity. Busy owners and managers will value the step-by-step guidance, scripts, and decision points that reduce hiring guesswork and strengthen retention. It's candid, actionable, and immediately usable.

Stacy Pursell, CPC, CERS
CEO and Executive Search Consultant
The VET Recruiter

With clarity and heart, *Your Veterinary Dream Team* offers veterinary leaders the tools they need to recruit with confidence and purpose. Gwen brings unmatched expertise, deep integrity, and genuine care for both practices and candidates to every page. Practice owners and managers will find this book both practical and inspiring, a guide grounded in ethics and wisdom from someone who truly understands the challenges and opportunities in veterinary recruiting.

Dani Rabwin, DVM
Founder and CEO
Ready, Vet, Go

Your Veterinary Dream Team is a must-read for any practice leader looking to strengthen their hiring approach. We all know the largest problem facing our profession is the need for great people at our hospitals, and Gwen Delavar delivers a clear, practical roadmap to address it. This book offers invaluable clarity, from step-by-step recruitment strategies to knowing when to bring in outside support. It will quickly become the go-to reference for building teams that not only deliver excellent medicine but also thrive together.

Kieran Mara
President and Chief Executive Officer
EVG Specialty

Building a veterinary hospital team is an art and a science. A great team provides great results. Gwen has created a guide to help every practice build their dream team. Tapping into years of experience helping practices to become successful, she has created a step-by-step resource that practice leadership can use to construct a team that works for all stakeholders: patients, clients, other team members, managers, doctors, and owners.

Peter Weinstein, DVM, MBA
President
PAW Consulting
Simple Solutions for Vets

This book highlights just how specialized and challenging veterinary recruiting has become. While tools and tactics are important, my experience has shown that true success lies in understanding the unique culture of each hospital and the long-term goals of each veterinarian. A placement isn't just about filling a role—it's about creating a partnership where both doctor and hospital can thrive for years to come.

What I appreciated most about this book is that it brings attention to a profession that often works quietly behind the scenes to support veterinarians and practice owners. For those of us who focus on privately owned hospitals, where culture and values matter deeply, the conversation this book starts is especially meaningful. It's a reminder that recruiting in veterinary medicine isn't simply transactional—it's about building relationships, fostering trust, and forming teams that last.

Victoria L. Travis, MS
President
Travis Veterinary Recruiters

Seldom does a book on recruiting delve into the real drivers of recruiting success, namely authenticity and forward planning, from giving a road map to next-generation recruiting and growth planning, to a no-nonsense look at platforms and optimization of recruiting avenues. This book truly does justice to Gwen's exceptional legacy and more than three decades of recruiting success know-how.

Kelly Cronin, MBA, VTS ECC, CVT, LVT
Senior Account Executive
International Hiring Made Simple

Gwen has captured the essence and finesse of veterinary recruiting in an elegant and eloquent style that makes it informative for hospital leadership and enjoyable to read, with thoughtful guidance, making ideas accessible and actionable. She has captured not just the why of hiring a recruiter but also gives a nuanced and balanced opinion on both internal and external recruiting. She provides the keys to a successful hospital recruiting system that helps a veterinary hospital to be proactive in finding and retaining ideal staff members, from associate veterinarians to assistants and CSRs. It's a must-read for anyone finding it difficult to recruit top veterinary talent, an essential resource for success in the rapidly shifting landscape of veterinary recruiting.

Rebecca Lakie, LVT
Pamela Harris, JD
VetNetAmerica

Due to staffing shortages in veterinary medicine, many new recruiters are popping up, looking to get a piece of the pie. However, picking the right recruiter can make all the difference in filling a position, not with just a body but with the right "fit" for your team. With over thirty years of professional veterinary recruiting experience, Gwen has written the ultimate guide to help practice owners and managers understand how professional recruiters work and how they get paid. If you need help deciding who can help you fill your position, I recommend reading Gwen's book. She takes the mystery out of the process.

Debbie Boone, BS, CVPM
President
Debbie Boone Consulting LLC

Throughout my fifteen-plus years of experience working with Gwen, I have consistently been impressed by her professionalism, insight, and strategic approach to matching candidates with opportunities that align with their experience, values, and long-term career objectives.

Gwen demonstrates a comprehensive understanding of both the clinical and organizational aspects of veterinary practice. She always takes the time to thoroughly understand the needs of each organization and each candidate's background and career goals, which in turn, promotes a higher percentage of long-term matches.

Gwen is genuinely invested in the success of the candidates and organizations she works with. Her ability to identify strong career fits and facilitate meaningful professional connections speaks to her expertise and dedication as a recruiter in this field.

Jason Bitting
Veterinary Leadership Professional

An insightful, down-to-earth guide for building stronger veterinary teams. *Your Veterinary Dream Team* offers practical strategies that actually work, from hiring well to knowing when to bring in outside help—a timely and valuable resource for today's leaders.

Alexandra (Allie) R. Ponkey, DVM
Intern
VCA West Los Angeles Animal Hospital

YOUR VETERINARY DREAM TEAM

YOUR VETERINARY DREAM TEAM

A Practical Guide to Attracting and Retaining Top Talent

GWENDOLYN LOWDER DELAVAR, CPVR

press 49

Press 49
4980 South Alma School Road
Suite 2-493
Chandler, Arizona 85248

Volume pricing is available for bulk orders from corporations, associations, and others. For bulk order details and media inquiries, please contact Press 49 at info@press49.com or 833.PRESS49 (833.773.7749).

FIRST EDITION

Library of Congress Control Number: 2025920035

ISBN (paperback): 978-1-953315-61-8
ISBN (eBook): 978-1-953315-62-5

BUS030000 BUSINESS & ECONOMICS / Human Resources & Personnel Management
BUS012020 BUSINESS & ECONOMICS / Careers / Interviewing
MED089000 MEDICAL / Veterinary Medicine / General

Interior and cover design by Medlar Publishing Solutions Pvt Ltd., India

Printed in the United States of America

Dedication

To Dr. Earl Gene Frie, DVM: You taught me how to be a veterinary technician and see veterinary practice as a business. You supported me on my path to becoming a veterinary practice manager and hospital administrator. I frequently utilize the tools you taught me.

To Mark Opperman, CVPM: You are a guiding light we lost too soon. Mark was instrumental to so many of us in the veterinary industry. Without his mentorship, friendship, and support, I would have struggled to get where I am today. I miss him always.

To Julia Janas: You are an amazing daughter, friend, and partner. You have been by my side since I first said, "What if we started a veterinary management business?" Not only did you help fund the business, but you were and are integral to every decision.

Table of Contents

Foreword

The veterinary profession stands at a crossroads. As demand for animal care surges and the scope of veterinary medicine expands, clinics and hospitals across the country face a growing challenge: recruiting and retaining talented veterinary professionals. This book arrives at a critical moment, offering insight, strategy, and inspiration for those tasked with building the future of veterinary teams.

Veterinary medicine is a calling but building a veterinary team—that's a craft. Over the years, as a former practice owner, practice operations and regulatory consultant for many practices around the country, I've learned that recruiting isn't just about résumés and interviews; it's about understanding the heart of a practice, the rhythm of a team, and the kind of care we want to deliver to our clients and their animals.

That's why I've always relied on Gwen.

Gwen has been my go-to recruiting partner for years, helping me and my clients find not just veterinarians and managers, but the right people—those who bring skill, compassion, and leadership to the table. Her insight into the veterinary profession is unmatched, and her ability to connect practices with professionals who truly fit is nothing short of remarkable.

This book, *Your Veterinary Dream Team*, is a reflection of that expertise. Gwen doesn't just know recruiting—she lives it. She understands the challenges, the nuances, and the urgency of finding great talent in a constantly evolving field. Whether you're a practice owner, medical director, associate veterinarian hospital administrator, or someone new to veterinary recruiting, you'll find wisdom here that's both practical and inspiring.

Gwen is the best in the business, and I'm honored to write this foreword for a book that I know will elevate how we think about recruiting in veterinary medicine.

Jan Woods
Former Practice Owner
Co-Owner and CEO, Ask Jan For Help LLC
CEO and President, Veterinary Management
and Marketing Specialists

Where It All Began

People often ask me, "How did you end up in veterinary recruiting?" Honestly, it wasn't part of some carefully designed master plan. Back in 1992, I was determined to build something of my own, and veterinary medicine turned out to be where my skills, curiosity, and persistence came together. Fast-forward to today, and not only have I built a thriving recruiting business, but in 2024, I also founded the National Veterinary Talent Acquisition Association™ (NVTAA™). It's been a journey filled with risks, learning curves, and plenty of laughter. Here's how it all began.

STARTING MY BUSINESS

Thirty-three years ago, armed with nothing more than a landline phone, a copy of the Yellow Pages (yes, the big book of ads we flipped through before Google existed), and a lot of nerve, I started cold-calling veterinary practice owners and managers. I'd introduce myself, explain my experience, and outline how I could help.

At that time, many practices weren't even computerized yet; the internet was just starting to make its way into everyday life.

My first opportunities weren't glamorous. Instead of recruiting, I was asked to collect overdue client payments for veterinary practices. I'd pick up stacks of records, spend hours on the phone, and earn a percentage of what I collected. Eventually, that opened doors to marketing projects for those same clients.

I registered my first DBA as Progressive Management Services (PMS), and let's just say veterinarians got a chuckle out of the acronym. I quickly pivoted and renamed it Progressive Veterinary Management Services™, later incorporating in California. Today, you know us as VetProCentral™.

I wasn't doing this alone, though. My daughter, Julia, was studying at San Diego State University and jumped right in to help. With her support, we bought a high-end laser printer (a big deal back then!) and started designing brochures, mailers, and logos for practices. I'm not sure the business would have survived those early years without her partnership. She's still by my side today, a partner, advisor, and recruiter.

A LEAP FORWARD

One of the smartest moves I made was reaching out to Mark Opperman, CVPM, a respected leader in veterinary practice management. I'd studied under him and told him I was ready to do more. His advice? Sponsor one of his seminars in San Diego.

He taught me how to plan the event from marketing to scheduling to securing a venue. We hosted his seminar, "It's What's Up Front That Counts," and it was a hit. I was too nervous to get on stage, so Mark introduced himself (and me) while I hid at the back. Still, that seminar helped me sign several new clients and gave me the confidence to take my business to the next level.

EXPANDING MY REACH

As time passed, Mark began sending me clients needing help hiring and training practice managers. At first, I'd travel to their clinics, serve as interim manager, and then train the new hire once they were on board. Over time, I realized much of the hiring could be done remotely, with me stepping in later for on-site training. This hybrid model worked beautifully and quickly became a success.

By the mid-90s, I met another recruiter in the veterinary space. We weren't competitors; instead, we teamed up, sharing candidates and opportunities. I sent her veterinarians; she sent me managers. I jokingly called us The Leading Ladies of Veterinary Recruiting™ because, for a while, we really were the only ones doing this work.

Eventually, clients asked if I could help hire veterinarians, too. At first, I hesitated because my background was in management, but I decided to expand my focus. That decision positioned me to meet the growing needs of the industry.

RUNNING A THRIVING BUSINESS

Today, our business has grown far beyond what I imagined when I first picked up that Yellow Pages. Based in San Diego, VetProCentral™ is powered by a team of recruiters, sourcers, an operations director, social media and marketing support, and an IT director. Together, we recruit exclusively in the veterinary field across the U.S., Canada, and even Hong Kong.

Looking back, the road wasn't easy, but every step (and misstep) taught me something valuable. And those lessons are the foundation of the guidance you'll find throughout this book.

Introduction: Why This Book, Why Now

Veterinary recruiting isn't what it used to be. It's tougher, faster-paced, and far more competitive than even a few years ago. If you've ever posted a job only to get crickets, lost a great candidate to another clinic at the last second, or felt like you were endlessly chasing the "right fit," you're not alone. The hiring landscape in veterinary medicine has shifted, and this book is here to help you shift with it.

This isn't theory—it's the hard-earned, practical advice from decades in the trenches of veterinary recruiting. My goal is to help you move from frustrated and reactive to confident and strategic in attracting, hiring, and retaining great people.

This book is written for practice managers, administrators, and in-house recruiters who are tired of feeling stuck. It's also for practice owners who've been dreaming of the day when they finally have a reliable, committed team. If that sounds like you, then you're in the right place.

Here's what you can expect:

- How to identify and attract candidates who align with your clinic's values and culture

- Which outreach strategies actually work (and which ones waste your time)

- Interviewing approaches that go beyond polished answers to uncover true motivation

- Ways to stand out in a crowded, competitive market

- Onboarding practices that don't just fill a seat but build long-term loyalty

One thing you won't find here? Endless statistics and salary tables. They're outdated by the time a book hits the shelves. Moreover, anecdotes, case studies, and unnecessary fluff are intentionally omitted. Instead, I get right to the point, which is my personality, as many who know me well will tell you, and I give you strategies you can adapt and apply no matter how the market shifts. A quick internet search will always be your friend if you want the latest numbers.

At its core, this is about more than filling roles. It's about building teams that allow your practice to thrive, reduce stress, and deliver the highest level of care. Recruiting in veterinary medicine isn't a side task anymore; it's a leadership skill. And by the time you've finished this book, you'll have a more precise roadmap for turning your hiring challenges into one of your greatest strengths.

So, whether you're hiring your first associate, trying to replace a burned-out team member, or scaling your practice for growth, consider this your guide to navigating the hiring journey with less stress, more clarity, and better results.

This primer offers a proven roadmap for building a high-performing, cohesive team without the guesswork.

CHAPTER 1

The State of Veterinary Hiring

Change is constant. The market will stabilize, but the
"new normal" is already here—embrace it.

Veterinary medicine is facing a hiring environment unlike any before it. Practices compete for a limited pool of talent, while outdated approaches to recruiting leave many clinics understaffed and overwhelmed. To thrive in this climate, leaders must understand today's labor market realities and rethink how they approach talent acquisition.

In this chapter, you will learn...

- An overview of the veterinary staffing crisis

- Why recruiting is now a leadership skill, not just an HR task

- Common hiring pitfalls in veterinary practices

- How to shift from reactive hiring to strategic recruitment

THE VETERINARY STAFFING CRISIS: A PERFECT STORM

Across the world, veterinary practices of all sizes are feeling the pressure of a staffing crisis that shows no sign of easing. Job boards are flooded with listings, while inboxes stay eerily quiet. You're not imagining it; the veterinary workforce has a severe mismatch between supply and demand.

This perfect storm has created intense competition for talent. It's no longer enough to assume a great candidate will come to you just because you have an opening. Veterinary professionals have options and make career decisions based on far more than salary alone.

You're already behind if you're still approaching hiring as an afterthought or only considering it when someone quits.

WHY RECRUITING IS NOW A CORE LEADERSHIP SKILL

Traditionally, hiring was treated as an administrative chore delegated to a practice manager or HR generalist, often with limited time and little strategy. But in today's labor market, recruiting is a leadership responsibility, not just a logistical task.

Think of it this way:

> To grow your practice, you need people to do the work.

> To maintain high standards of care, you need consistent, committed team members.

You need a stable, functional team to reduce stress and improve morale.

None of these goals is possible without strong recruiting and retention practices. That means leaders—whether owners, medical directors, or practice managers—must take ownership of talent acquisition and view it as mission-critical.

Today's most successful practices are led by people who embrace their role as talent magnets. They're not just reacting to open roles; they're thinking six months, one year, even two years ahead. Recruiting isn't a sprint; it's an ongoing investment in the practice's future.

COMMON HIRING PITFALLS IN VETERINARY PRACTICES

Before we look at solutions, it's helpful to recognize what's not working. Many veterinary clinics fall into one or more of these traps:

Waiting Too Long to Start the Search

When a team member gives notice, panic sets in. A rushed process often leads to poor decisions, missed red flags, or unfilled roles that overburden the remaining team.

Generic, Uninspired Job Ads

"Fast-paced clinic seeks dedicated veterinarian" isn't a compelling invitation. It's white noise in a sea of sameness. It will be ignored if your job posting looks like everyone else's.

Relying Solely on Job Boards

"Posting and praying" isn't a strategy. In a competitive market, passive recruiting won't cut it. The best candidates often need to be sourced and persuaded.

Undervaluing Culture Fit and Long-Term Potential

Focusing only on clinical skills and availability leads to turnover. Shared values and growth opportunities are what keep people long-term.

Inconsistent or Unprofessional Interview Processes

Disorganized interviews, unclear expectations, or delays in decision-making frustrate candidates and make even the best practice look unattractive.

If you've experienced any of these pitfalls, you're not alone. The good news is that they're all fixable. With a shift in mindset and intentional systems, you can go from frustrated to confident in your hiring efforts.

FROM REACTIVE TO STRATEGIC: THE NEW RECRUITMENT MINDSET

Strategic recruitment is about being proactive, intentional, and consistent. It means designing a system that runs even when you're not actively hiring. It's about building relationships before you need them and creating a workplace people want to join.

Here's how the shift looks in practice:

Reactive Hiring	Strategic Hiring
Hiring in response to a resignation	Hiring in anticipation of future needs
Posting the same generic job ad everywhere	Customizing messaging for your ideal candidate
Scrambling to fill a role quickly	Actively sourcing candidates via databases, social media, networking, and outreach
Letting HR handle everything	Building a bench of potential future hires
Focusing on clinical skills only	Hiring for clinical skills, values, fit, and growth potential

By adopting a strategic mindset, you'll not just solve staffing problems; you'll shape your practice's future. A thoughtful plan reduces stress, boosts morale, and fosters a cohesive team culture. Most importantly, it puts you back in control instead of worrying about who will send the next resignation email.

WHAT'S AHEAD

This book walks you through the recruitment process, from defining your ideal hire to effectively onboarding new team members.

You don't need to become a full-time recruiter to succeed. But you do need to become a strategic one.

KEY TAKEAWAY

The veterinary hiring crisis is real, but it doesn't have to define your future. By treating recruiting as a core leadership skill, avoiding common pitfalls, and shifting from reactive to strategic hiring, you can build a stable, resilient team that supports your practice for years to come.

CHAPTER 2

What (and Who) Is a Veterinary Recruiter?

Headhunter, recruiter, talent scout—call me whatever you like,
just don't forget to call me.

The success of any veterinary practice depends on its people, and hiring the right people requires someone who can focus fully on finding, attracting, and placing them. That's where veterinary recruiters come in. Whether internal or external, recruiters navigate complex hiring landscapes, assess candidate fit, and help practices build strong, sustainable teams.

Understanding who recruiters are, what they do, and how they operate is critical for practice leaders who want to turn recruiting into a true strategic advantage.

In this chapter, you will learn...

- The definition and core responsibilities of a veterinary recruiter and how the role can vary across different types of practices

- The differences between internal and external veterinary recruiters, including the main recruiting models used in the industry

- Who veterinary recruiters typically report to and how the role fits into different organizational structures

- How veterinary recruiters are compensated, from salaried in-house positions to contingency and subscription-based external models

DEFINING THE ROLE

Veterinary recruiters are rapidly becoming one of the most critical roles in veterinary practices today. As practice owners and corporate teams struggle to meet patient demand amid a national workforce shortage, the ability to consistently attract and hire qualified candidates has become a true competitive advantage.

A veterinary recruiter's primary focus is to help fill positions within veterinary hospitals, most often veterinarians, leadership, and credentialed technicians but sometimes support staff as well. Their work includes identifying potential candidates, assessing fit, communicating the practice's values and offerings, and facilitating the hiring process in partnership with practice leadership.

While that description may sound straightforward, the role varies significantly depending on the organization's size, structure, and priorities. In a large corporate-owned hospital group, a recruiter may be part of a regional or national talent acquisition team, often specializing in sourcing while leaving interviews and onboarding to local leaders. In a midsize or independently owned practice, however, the recruiter may wear multiple hats: posting jobs, screening applicants, coordinating interviews, and even assisting with onboarding or employer branding.

Some recruiters come from HR backgrounds; others transition from operations, sales, or even the clinical side of veterinary medicine. Their paths differ, but the goal remains the same: connect the right candidates with the right opportunities and help practices build sustainable teams.

A DAY (OR A YEAR) IN THE LIFE

The day-to-day work of a veterinary recruiter might include writing and updating job ads, posting to job boards, reaching out to passive candidates, screening applicants by phone or video, and managing résumés. Responsiveness is key, as top candidates often move quickly or disappear just as fast.

Over the course of a quarter of a year, recruiters may analyze sourcing results, attend job fairs, build relationships with veterinary schools, or refine job descriptions to better attract talent. On an annual time frame, they may contribute to workforce planning, forecasting staffing needs based on turnover or growth goals, and supporting broader efforts like employer branding or retention strategies.

Recruiters are also storytellers. They help shape a practice's public image by communicating culture, growth opportunities, compensation philosophy, and mentorship offerings. To succeed, a recruiter must not only understand the veterinary industry at large but also the specific practice they represent.

INTERNAL VS. EXTERNAL VETERINARY RECRUITERS

Internal recruiters are employed directly by the hospital, group, or organization they represent. Their loyalty lies exclusively with the practice, and their work often involves deeper collaboration with medical and administrative teams, as well as a stronger grasp of culture fit and long-term hiring success.

External recruiters, by contrast, are independent contractors, consultants, or employees of third-party recruiting firms. Practices often engage them when internal bandwidth is limited or a critical hire proves difficult. External recruiters may work via contingency models (paid only upon a successful hire), flat-fee arrangements (a set amount regardless of outcome), or subscription-based models (ongoing services for a monthly rate).

While external recruiters may juggle multiple clients, experienced professionals often specialize in veterinary recruiting and can be valuable allies, especially for hard-to-fill roles or national searches.

Choosing between internal and external recruiting, or using both, is a strategic decision based on goals, budget, and internal capabilities. Each model offers advantages, and many practices successfully use both at different stages.

WHO DO VETERINARY RECRUITERS REPORT TO?

Reporting structures vary. In larger systems, recruiters may report to a director of talent acquisition, human resources, or operations. In smaller practices, they might report to the practice manager, hospital administrator, or even the owner/medical director.

In many independent hospitals, there is no dedicated recruiter at all. Recruiting often falls to practice owners, managers, or lead veterinarians, who are already balancing clinical and administrative responsibilities. While this can work short-term, it underscores the need for dedicated recruiting support, whether internal or external, to ensure hiring doesn't get neglected during busy seasons.

HOW VETERINARY RECRUITERS ARE COMPENSATED

Internal recruiters are usually salaried employees and may earn bonuses for hiring performance, retention, or organizational goals. In some practices, recruiting is only part of a broader HR or operations role, so compensation reflects those combined duties.

External recruiters are compensated through structured agreements with the hiring practice. This could mean contingency fees, flat-fee contracts, or subscription-based models. Fees often vary based on role complexity and market competitiveness. (Later in the book, we'll explore these compensation models in greater detail.)

BRINGING IT ALL TOGETHER

Whether internal or external, full-time or part of a larger role, veterinary recruiters are essential to the success and sustainability of a practice. Their work goes far beyond filling vacancies; they shape the team, influence culture, and ultimately impact the client and patient experience.

As the veterinary workforce continues to evolve, so will the recruiter's role. Understanding who recruiters are and how they operate is the first step toward building a strong, strategic hiring function.

Now that you have a clear picture of a veterinary recruiter, the next step is to define what "right" looks like for your practice. In the next chapter, we'll focus on clinically, culturally, and personally identifying your ideal hire so your recruiting efforts have the clarity and direction needed to succeed.

CHAPTER 3

Defining Your Ideal Hire

Unicorns are rare and hard to manage. Let's find the right person for your team instead.

Successful hiring starts long before posting a job ad or scheduling an interview. The foundation of every great hire is clarity about the role, the skills and traits required, and the type of person who will thrive in your practice. Without this focus, even talented candidates may struggle to fit, and your team risks turnover, frustration, and lost productivity.

In this chapter, you will learn...

- How to build role clarity before you advertise

- Which traits and qualifications matter for different positions

- How to create candidate personas to guide your search

THE COST OF THE WRONG HIRE

Most hiring mistakes don't happen during interviews. They happen before a job is ever posted. When managers rush to replace someone without clearly defining their needs, they chase warm bodies instead of building strong, cohesive teams.

Hiring someone who doesn't fit your team's values, culture, or expectations is costly, financially, emotionally, and operationally. A bad hire often leads to...

- Decreased team morale

- Client complaints or reduced service quality

- Higher turnover, as colleagues burn out or feel frustrated

- Wasted time and resources on training that doesn't stick

- Workflow disruptions, especially in small teams

Recruiting isn't just about filling a gap. It's about strengthening your team. Hiring the right person is a strategic decision that affects your practice's culture, client satisfaction, and bottom line for years to come.

Step 1: Identify the Real Needs of the Role

Consider this scenario: Your associate veterinarian is leaving. The obvious solution might seem to be replacing them with another veterinarian, but pause. Is there a need for more coverage, improved client communication, or someone experienced in urgent cases? Could better utilization of your existing team reduce the need for a replacement? Ask yourself...

- What are the essential duties of this position?

- What hours or shifts need coverage?

- Are there gaps this hire should fill that weren't addressed before?

- How will this role interact with other team members?

- Will hiring for this position require adding more support staff?

Pro Tip: Review the last six to twelve months of feedback or performance evaluations for the outgoing team member. What worked well? What didn't? Let that guide your requirements for the next hire.

Step 2: Create a Candidate Persona

A candidate persona is a snapshot of the person who will succeed in your environment. Think of it as a filter that helps you prioritize the best match. Ask...

- What motivates this person?

- What kind of culture or leadership style do they thrive under?

- What would excite them about joining your practice specifically?

Examples of Positions and Ideal Traits	
Position	**Ideal Traits**
Associate veterinarian	Confident communicator, enjoys mentorship, experienced
Registered veterinary technician	Detail-oriented, calm under pressure, compassionate
Customer service representative	Tech-savvy, multitasker, warm and welcoming

Step 3: Define Non-Negotiables vs. Nice-to-Haves

It's important to distinguish between must-have requirements and wish-list qualities. Unrealistically high bars can exclude candidates who could grow into the role.

Non-Negotiables	Nice to Have's
• Active state license	• Internship-trained
• At least one year of experience	• Exotic experience
• Strong communication skills	• Familiarity with your software
• Team-oriented attitude	• Interest in surgery

Be honest. What can be trained, and what cannot? You can teach medical record protocols, but kindness under pressure is non-negotiable.

Step 4: Clarify What You're Offering

Attracting the right candidates isn't just about what you need. It's also about what you provide…

- Schedule flexibility

- Supportive team culture

- Mentorship and growth opportunities

- Continuing Education allowance and career development

- Work-life balance policies

- Clear expectations and communication

- Competitive salaries and benefits aligned with today's candidates' values

It's not about being everything to everyone. It's about being the right fit for the right person.

Step 5: Align the Team

Before launching your search, ensure everyone involved in hiring is aligned. Misalignment can create confusion, delays, and mixed signals to candidates. Discuss and agree on…

- The role's purpose and expectations

- Key qualities and traits prioritized

- Responsibilities in the hiring process

- How candidates will be evaluated consistently

When the hiring team is aligned, the process is smoother, faster, and more cohesive for your team and candidates.

FROM CLARITY COMES CONFIDENCE

Defining your ideal hire reduces risk, shortens time-to-hire, and sets your new team member up for success from day one. More importantly, it shifts your mindset from desperation to discernment. Hiring isn't just a function. It's a filter. The right people are far more likely to come through when that filter is clear.

CHAPTER 4

Crafting a Magnetic Employer Brand

Competition is fierce. Don't blend in. Stand out.

Now that you know who you're looking for, it's time to ensure candidates know why they should work for you. This chapter will focus on building an employer brand that attracts the right people and sets your practice apart in a crowded market.

In this chapter, you will learn...

- How to audit your current brand presence

- Telling your practice's story in a way that attracts talent

- Leveraging your website and social media

WHY EMPLOYER BRANDING MATTERS MORE THAN EVER

Employer branding isn't just for large veterinary corporations. It's critical for practices of all sizes. In veterinary medicine, your reputation as an employer is your most powerful recruiting asset or your most significant liability. Candidates are asking the same questions everywhere:

- What's it like to work here?

- What are the mission, vision, and goals of the practice?

- Will I be supported, respected, and valued?

- Is this a team I want to join, not just a job I want to do?

In a saturated hiring market, candidates are drawn to practices where culture feels aligned, the mission is clear, and people seem genuinely happy. Your employer brand is not about perks or flashy facilities. It's your practice personality, and it exists whether you've consciously shaped it or not.

WHAT IS AN EMPLOYER BRAND?

Your employer brand is the overall perception of your veterinary practice as a place to work, including experiences, expectations, and perceptions of current and prospective employees.

Employer brand: your aspirational image—the story you want to tell about your practice

Employer brand perception: how others actually perceive your practice as a workplace

Think of it as your practice personality, a chance to tell your story before someone else does. Your employer brand is shaped by…

- Reputation in the local veterinary community

- Online presence (website, social media, job ads, reviews)

- Word of mouth from former employees and externs

- Interview and onboarding experience

- Day-to-day team dynamics

THE MYTH OF "WE'RE A GREAT PLACE TO WORK"

Every practice thinks it's a great place to work. Simply saying it is not enough. To stand out, speak directly to what your ideal candidate cares about and show—not just tell—why your practice is different.

Ask yourself…

- What do current team members love most about working here?

- What kind of people thrive in our environment?

- What are we genuinely proud of, and what are we still working on?

A strong employer brand doesn't pretend to be perfect. It reflects your practice's values, growth mindset, and team culture with authenticity.

Step 1: Audit Your Current Employer Brand

Before promoting your practice to job seekers, understand how you're currently perceived.

Online Presence Check:

- Is your website up-to-date, visually appealing, and easy to navigate?

- Do you have a careers page that explains why someone should join your team?

- Do your social media accounts reflect a positive, engaged team culture?

- Are employee and client reviews accurate and positive?

Internal Culture Check:

- Would your current team recommend your practice to a friend as an employer?

- Do you celebrate wins, support growth, and address burnout and mental health?

- Are communication, expectations, and leadership consistent?

Consider an anonymous internal survey for real insights.

Reputation Check:

- What do former employees say about you?

- Do you have positive relationships with local veterinary schools and associations?

- Are you known for mentorship, learning, or innovation?

You don't need to score perfectly, but you do need to know where you stand. Candidates research practices carefully, and a weak brand can cost you top talent.

Step 2: Tell Your Story With Intention

A compelling employer brand tells a story about why your practice exists and the people you want to attract.

Answer these key questions:

- Mission: What drives your team? Why do you exist beyond profit?

- Culture: What values do you live by? How do you support each other?

- Vision: What are you building? How do new hires fit into that journey?

- Team: Who works here now, and what do they say about the experience?

Example of a branded statement:

> *Riverside Animal Urgent Care is building a next-generation urgent care team focused on collaboration, mentorship, and sustainable scheduling. Excellent medicine starts with a supported team, and we hire for kindness, curiosity, and calm under pressure.*

Compare that to a generic job posting:

> *Fast-paced clinic seeking experienced ER veterinarian.*

The difference is clear.

Step 3: Show, Don't Just Tell

Give candidates a behind-the-scenes look at your practice. Ideas include...

Team Spotlights: Interview team members and share on your website or social media.

Client Testimonials: Post client success stories, with permission.

Day in the Life Posts: Show teamwork and daily shifts via photos, videos, or reels.

Values in Action: Highlight diversity, wellness initiatives, or community outreach.

Externship Feedback: Share student experiences to show mentorship opportunities.

Celebrations: Highlight birthdays, work anniversaries, and wins.

Authenticity wins over professional polish. Use your phone and be real. Always secure signed permissions for clients or employee photos.

Step 4: Consistency Is Everything

Every touchpoint, from job ads to onboarding, should reflect your brand. Inconsistencies create confusion and undermine trust.

Touchpoint	What It Should Convey
Job ad	Clear, specific tone reflecting culture
Website and careers page	Why the practice is worth joining
Social media accounts	Proof of team engagement and values in action
Interview process	Respect for candidates' time and transparent communication
Onboarding	Continuation of promises made during hiring

Step 5: Treat Your Employer Brand as a Living Asset

Your employer brand evolves with every hire, social post, externship, and team meeting. Treat it intentionally and build it over time.

If you're not where you want to be yet, start small. One step at a time is progress.

Your employer brand is more than a logo or slogan. It's the story candidates experience before, during, and after the hiring process. You'll attract candidates who align with your culture and values by auditing your current brand, telling your story with intention, showing authenticity, and staying consistent.

CHAPTER 5

Writing Job Posts That Stand Out

"Post and pray" isn't a strategy. Be authentic, be clear, and track your results.

Now that you've shaped your employer brand, it's time to leverage it. In this chapter, we'll break down how to write job ads that don't just describe a position but inspire the right candidates to apply.

In this chapter, you will learn...

- The anatomy of a compelling job ad

- Examples of effective vs. ineffective veterinary job descriptions

- Common mistakes that drive candidates away

- Where and how to post for maximum reach

WHY MOST JOB ADS DON'T WORK

Open any veterinary job board, and you'll see countless ads using the same tired language:

> "Busy practice seeking dedicated, compassionate veterinarian."

> "Fast-paced clinic. Competitive salary. Great team."

These descriptions are vague, interchangeable, and uninspiring. They might check the box but don't speak to the candidates you want to attract. Worse, they don't reflect the personality, culture, or values of your practice that you worked so hard to build. (See Chapter 4.)

In a market flooded with options, bland job ads are invisible job ads. The good news? You don't need to be a marketing expert to write compelling job posts. You just need a clear structure, human language, and intentional messaging.

THE PURPOSE OF A JOB POST

Your job ad isn't a complete history of your practice, nor a list of every task. Its purpose is to start a conversation. A great ad should...

- Capture attention

- Spark curiosity

- Connect with values

- Make it easy for candidates to take the next step

Think of your job ad like a dating profile. Speak like a human, not a robot. You're not just looking for someone who can do the job. You want someone who wants to do the job with your practice and team.

ANATOMY OF A HIGH-PERFORMING JOB POST

1. Headline That Grabs Attention

This is your billboard. Be specific, bold, and human.

Examples:

> "Tired of Burnout? We're Building Something Different in Small Animal ER"

> "Want to Love Vet Med Again? Join Our Fear-Free Team in Austin"

> "Flexible Veterinarian Role with Mentorship, No Sundays, and Actual Lunch Breaks"

Avoid:

> "Veterinarian Wanted"

> "Associate Veterinarian Position"

> "Full-Time Vet Opportunity"

2. Hook/Opening Paragraph

Start with empathy or vision. Speak directly to what your ideal candidate might be thinking or feeling.

Example:

> "You didn't go to veterinary school to burn out. You went because you love medicine, connections with people and pets, and making a difference. At Stone Creek Veterinary, we get it, and we're building a team that brings joy back to the profession."

3. About the Role

Be clear but concise. Highlight scope, schedule, support, flexibility, and types of clients/community.

Example:

> "We're looking for a full-time Veterinarian (new graduates welcome!) to join our three-doctor small animal team. You'll see a mix of wellness, urgent care, and soft-tissue surgery, with the freedom to pursue your clinical passions."

Tip: Embed a short "a day in the life" video if possible.

4. About the Team and Culture

Here's where your employer brand shines. Share what sets your team apart.

Example:

> "We're a tight-knit group of animal lovers who support each other fiercely. Our techs are experienced, our leadership is transparent, and our favorite thing is lunchtime trivia (yes, really). We believe in growth, kindness, and giving everyone a voice."

Avoid vague phrases like: "Great team environment."

5. Information About City/State/Area

Highlight notable aspects: schools, indoor/outdoor activities, sports, and professional opportunities.

6. What the Candidate Will Get

Outline benefits and perks, beyond salary.

Examples:

- $130,000 to $160,000 salary (no production pressure)

- Four-day workweek, no weekends

- $2,500 Continuing Education + mentorship funds

- Generous PTO + mental health days

- Health insurance

- Paid parental leave

- Reproductive health care

- Relocation/signing bonus

- American Veterinary Medical Association (AVMA), Veterinary Information Network (VIN), and Fear Free certifications paid
- Supportive, values-driven leadership

State clearly if you're flexible on schedule or open to new graduates and early career candidates.

7. Who This Role Is Perfect For

Filter for traits and values, not just qualifications.

Example:

> "You'll thrive here if you value collaboration over competition, take pride in your medicine, and believe a good laugh belongs in every shift. We're big on growth, low on ego, and serious about kindness."

8. Call to Action

Make applying simple, friendly, and approachable.

Example:

> "Ready to find out if we're your next home? Reach out directly to [Your Name and Email]. List your cell for call/text. Tell us what you're looking for, even if your résumé isn't perfect. We'd love to hear from you."

Pro Tip: Direct candidates to a simple website career page. Avoid long application forms; they discourage applicants. Ask for name, title, contact information, and a curriculum vitae/résumé upload button. Ensure that an email message is automatically sent to you when anyone applies and that you reply in a timely manner.

Bonus: Visuals and Personality

Add photos, videos, or short team tours. Authenticity builds trust and signals that this is a real job post. Always get signed permission before posting employees' or clients' names and/or photos.

COMMON JOB POST MISTAKES TO AVOID

- Too long, dry, or formal

- Listing every possible task or requirement

- Burying the best parts of the job

- Omitting contact info

- Making the process too formal

- Using vague phrases like "fast-paced" or "must work under pressure"

WHERE AND HOW TO POST

Platforms to consider:

- Industry-specific job boards

- Professional social media (veterinary-specific groups, veterinary communities)

- Veterinary university career sites plus alumni sites

- Clinic website and social media

- Email newsletters, referral programs, and partnerships with veterinary schools

Social Media Frequency

Aim for three to five weekly posts (weekday mornings are recommended). Mix photos, videos, and updates to maintain consistency, and track engagement to refine your posting strategy.

Your job ad is more than a checklist; it's an invitation. You're not just hiring a skillset but inviting someone to join your story. Write like it matters because it does.

CHAPTER 6

Sourcing Candidates Beyond Job Boards

If everyone is fishing in the same pond, it's time to find a new lake.

Finding the right veterinary team member isn't just about posting a job ad and hoping for the best; it's about going out and finding them before you need them. In today's competitive talent market, the best candidates are often already employed, and waiting until a position opens can leave you scrambling to fill it. This chapter shifts your mindset from reactive hiring to proactive recruiting, giving you the tools to identify, connect with, and nurture relationships with potential candidates long before they apply.

In this chapter, you'll learn how to…

- Understand why "post and pray" hiring fails in today's veterinary job market and how sourcing both active and passive candidates creates a stronger, more competitive talent pipeline

- Apply proactive sourcing strategies, including social media outreach, school partnerships, referrals, Boolean search techniques, and alumni networks, to uncover hidden veterinary talent

- Start early and build relationships over time so you're never scrambling to hire under pressure

- Use practical systems and best practices for tracking candidates, staying organized, and turning one conversation today into a great hire months from now

Now that you know how to write an ad that attracts the right people, it's time to find them. Discover proactive sourcing strategies, from outreach to referrals to social media, so you're not waiting and hoping the right candidate happens to see your post.

- Passive vs. active candidates: how to reach both

- Sourcing Early

- Using social media, school career centers, and more

- Direct outreach script

- Using Boolean Search

- Using AI

WHY "POST AND PRAY" DOESN'T WORK ANYMORE

There was a time when you could post a veterinary job online and wait for the résumés to roll in. That time is over.

If your only strategy is posting a job and waiting, you're missing out on eighty percent of the talent pool. In today's talent market, the best candidates aren't browsing job boards; they're already working elsewhere. They might be open to the right opportunity, but they're not actively looking.

ACTIVE AND PASSIVE CANDIDATES

When recruiting in the veterinary industry, it's essential to understand the difference between active and passive candidates and how to reach each group effectively. Active candidates are actively searching for a new position, browsing job boards, submitting applications, and are likely open to immediate conversations. These candidates are easier to find but also tend to apply to multiple roles, which means competition is high. On the other hand, passive candidates are currently employed and not actively looking, but they may be open to the right opportunity if it speaks to their goals or solves a pain point. Reaching active candidates requires strong job postings in visible places like job boards, industry forums, and social media. Reaching passive candidates demands a more strategic approach: building relationships over time, leveraging professional networks, using tools on social media to initiate direct outreach, and crafting personalized messages that spark curiosity and speak to their values. The most successful recruiting strategies address both groups, combining visibility with thoughtful engagement.

This is where sourcing comes in.

Sourcing means proactively finding, engaging, and building relationships with potential candidates before they apply. It's the difference between fishing with a hook and casting a net.

Why is it important to source early?

Sourcing early is one of the most critical strategies in successful veterinary recruiting. Waiting until a position is vacant—or worse, until it's already causing stress on the team—puts you in reactive mode, limiting your options and increasing the likelihood of a rushed or poor hire. The veterinary talent pool is competitive and limited, and great candidates are often off the market quickly. By sourcing early, you give yourself time to build relationships, nurture passive candidates, and create a warm pipeline of potential hires before the need becomes urgent. Early sourcing also allows you to be more intentional in your selection process, aligning candidates with your culture, clinical philosophy, and long-term goals. Simply put, proactive sourcing shifts recruiting from a last-minute scramble to a strategic advantage.

THE MINDSET SHIFT: FROM HIRING TO RECRUITING

Most hiring managers wait until there's an urgent need to start recruiting. By then, the clock is ticking, the team is short-staffed, and every week without a hire feels more stressful. It also means lost revenue for the practice.

Strategic sourcing flips the script. You're not waiting for people to come to you. You're building a pipeline of future teammates before the need becomes critical.

That means…

- Reaching out early

- Building relationships over time

- Staying top of mind—even if someone isn't ready to move yet

This approach is especially effective in veterinary medicine, where relationships, reputation, and referrals matter just as much as job titles.

WHERE TO FIND HIDDEN TALENT

Veterinary candidates aren't just sitting on job boards. They are working across town, graduating next semester, or quietly browsing job boards and social media without hitting "apply." If you want to find the best candidates before your competitors do, you have to think beyond traditional postings and learn to source proactively. In this section, you'll discover eight practical and proven strategies to uncover hidden veterinary talent, from smart social media sleuthing to tapping into your own client base. Whether you're new to recruiting or looking to level up your efforts, this roadmap will help you build a steady pipeline of candidates before the need becomes urgent.

1. Social Media

Search for the following across various social media platforms:

- Veterinarians and veterinary techs by title and city

- Veterinary school students and graduates by class year and specific veterinary schools

- People working at nearby practices, shelters, or mobile services

Pro Tip: Reach out to people with personalized messages, not copy-paste templates.

Example:

> "Hi, Dr. Lee. I came across your profile while looking for values-driven veterinarians in the Dallas area. I manage a clinic that's doing things a bit differently, and I'd love to connect in case the timing's ever right for a conversation. No pressure. I just wanted to say hi!"

2. Old-School Outreach with a Modern Edge

In today's veterinary recruiting world, most communication happens through digital means, including leaning heavily on social media. But sometimes, the unexpected is what stands out. Target marketing to a select group can be effective. A handwritten note, a personalized card, or a thoughtful letter can cut through the digital clutter and leave a lasting impression.

Direct mail isn't a high-volume recruiting tool any longer, but it can be a powerful tool when used selectively. Consider sending a personal note or well-crafted letter to…

- A specialist or senior veterinarian who probably receives dozens of digital inquiries each week

- A candidate you've already spoken with, as a follow-up to reinforce sincerity

- Someone you want to build a long-term relationship with, even if they're not ready to move now

- Someone who isn't active on social media

This "old-school" touch shows authenticity and effort—qualities that resonate deeply in a relationship-driven profession like veterinary medicine.

3. Veterinary Groups

They tend to be full of opportunities. Join the following types of groups:

- Veterinary-specific job and networking groups

- Technician-focused or veterinary management groups and specialty groups

- Externship and mentorship pages

- Local or regional vet circles

Don't spam. Instead, engage with posts, build credibility, and share meaningful updates from your clinic.

Post ideas:

- A behind-the-scenes photo plus "We're growing! Message me if you want to chat!"

- "We're hosting externs this summer. DM me if you know a student who'd be a great fit."

- A win from your team: "This is why we love what we do."

4. Veterinary Schools, Externship and Internship Programs

Developing relationships with schools is a long game but is a game worth playing. Here are the steps for doing so:

- Reach out to career services or faculty members

- Offer to speak on panels, host lunch-and-learns, or mentor students

- Attend career fairs at veterinary schools and veterinary tech schools

- Sponsor events at veterinary-specific meetings

- Speak at veterinary schools and clubs

- Create externship and shadowing opportunities

- Follow up with every student who rotates through; these are warm leads

Remember that you're not just filling a role. You're creating a reputation as a clinic that grows talent.

5. Referrals from Your Team

Your current team knows who's good at what they do and who's looking. Encourage staff to recommend former classmates, friends, or colleagues. But don't just ask once and forget it. Build a simple, repeatable referral process.

Ideas for doing this are as follows:

- Offer a referral bonus (cash, gift cards, extra PTO) for referred candidates who are hired

- Create a quarterly "referral round-up" challenge

Pro Tip: Celebrate successful referrals publicly.

6. Your Clients

Yes, really. Veterinary clients are often well-connected and love to support practices they trust.

Ways to tap into your client base:

- Add "we're hiring!" to your email signature, website banner, newsletter, and appointment screen. Be certain this is clickable and leads to your website, where they can apply or recommend a referral

- Create a referral incentive for client recommendations (e.g., a one-hundred-dollar account credit if you hire someone they refer)

7. Boolean Searches on the Internet

Boolean search writing is a skill that top recruiters need to know to achieve more meaningful search results. However, Boolean searches are becoming less central in veterinary talent sourcing because modern AI tools now interpret intent rather than relying solely on strict keyword patterns. With AI embedded into most recruiting platforms, search engines can understand context, match transferable skills, and surface qualified veterinary candidates even when their profiles don't contain exact Boolean terms.

It remains a valuable tool for understanding and utilizing effectively. A Boolean search string can look confusing and complex, but there are only five elements to understand:

AND   any search terms that follow an AND command must appear in the result

OR   provides options; usage allows you to create a list of possibilities for which only one match is important

NOT   the command of exclusion

( ) and [ ]   ( ) parentheses and [ ] brackets are not the same in a Boolean search; parentheses ( ) are used to group terms and specify the order of operations, while brackets [ ] can be used similarly for grouping or may have a separate function, such as case sensitivity in some specific search engines. Both parentheses and brackets override the default operator precedence (e.g., AND before OR), ensuring that the enclosed terms are processed first.

" "   used to capture a phrase that means each word is treated separately

Examples of Boolean Searches:

1. Small animal general veterinarian, San Diego, CA

("DVM" OR "Doctor of Veterinary Medicine" OR veterinarian) AND ("small animal" OR "companion animal") AND ("San Diego" OR "San Diego County") AND ("general practice" OR GP OR "wellness care")

2. Shelter veterinarian, Houston, TX

("shelter veterinarian" OR "shelter medicine" OR "animal shelter" OR "high-volume spay neuter" OR "community medicine") AND (veterinarian OR DVM OR "Doctor of Veterinary Medicine") AND ("Houston" OR "Harris County" OR "TX")

3. Veterinary technician, ER practice, Palm Beach, FL

["veterinary technician" OR "vet tech" OR CVT OR LVT OR RVT] AND ["emergency" OR "ER" OR "urgent care" OR "critical care"] AND [Palm Beach OR "Palm Beach FL" OR "Palm Beach County" OR "South Florida"]

8. Alumni Networks

Veterinary and veterinary technical school alumni groups often have private job boards, email lists, or social networks to tap into to find talent.

Reach out to…

- Alumni offices

- Class social media groups

You're not just asking candidates to apply; you're building visibility in these graduate networks.

HOW TO REACH OUT WITHOUT SOUNDING PUSHY

Outreach messages should feel personal, relevant, and non-transactional. Avoid the "hard sell."

Here's a basic formula:

1. Share a genuine compliment or mention a shared connection.

2. Explain why you're reaching out.

3. Briefly describe the top priorities, values, and benefits of the practice.

4. Provide a clear, no-pressure invitation to connect.

Example:

> "Hey, Gwen. I saw you're a licensed tech with ER experience, and I was impressed by the passion in your posts. I help run a clinic that's working hard to protect work-life balance and mental wellness in emergency medicine. Totally understand if you're happy where you are, but if you're ever curious, I'd love to tell you about what we're building. No pressure at all!"

The goal isn't to "convert" someone. It's to open the door for a real conversation.

BEST PRACTICES FOR SOURCING CANDIDATES

If you want sourcing to pay off, treat it like a system, not a scramble.

Simple ways to stay organized...

- Use a spreadsheet, an applicant tracking system (ATS), or a customer relationship management platform (CRM) to track contacts and follow-ups.

- Set reminders to check back in one to two months (or sooner, depending on their responses to you).

- Keep notes on each candidate's goals, timing, or concerns.

- Track your referral program and refine it to keep it effective and efficient.

The most effective sourcing happens when you…

- Block out time every week (even just thirty minutes)

- Focus on relationship-building, not "filling a role"

- Stay visible, responsive, and human

You are a recruiter, so think as the best of us do: Your best hire six months from now might be someone you reached out to today. This is how veterinary practices go from reactive hiring to proactive talent building.

CHAPTER 7

Using Social Media in Veterinary Recruiting

No plan? No results. Create a strategy first. Make the post second.

Social media involves more than just posting jobs. It's about building relationships, boosting your employer brand, and reaching passive candidates where they spend time. Social media isn't just a broadcast tool. Learn to use it effectively to hire.

In this chapter, you will learn how to...

- Amplify your employer brand, humanize your team, and make candidates feel like they know you before they apply

- Create connection and visibility that lead to better hires

CHOOSE THE RIGHT PLATFORMS

Not all social media platforms serve the same audience or purpose. Choosing the right ones allows you to spend your time wisely and tailor your messaging for the best results.

Platform	Best for...	Use it to...	Pro Tip
LinkedIn	DVMs, specialists, hospital leaders, practice managers, and high-performing veterinary technicians	• Post detailed job listings and thought leadership content • Connect with veterinary professionals and alumni from specific schools • Join or create niche veterinary recruiting or management groups • Message passive candidates directly with personalized notes	Your personal LinkedIn profile should reflect your clinic's brand. Share hiring wins, team culture, or even interview tips.
Facebook	Veterinary technicians, support staff, CSRs, and local or community-based candidates	• Join veterinary-specific groups (e.g., Vet Tech Nation or VetMed Moms) • Post photos of your team, events, or job openings • Run ads targeting location, job title, or interests • Create or manage a practice page that highlights culture and career opportunities	Follow each group's rules. Many don't allow job postings but do permit networking or referrals in comments or specific threads.
Instagram	Younger veterinarians, vet students, and techs who are drawn to visual and emotional content	• Share short reels or stories of daily clinic life • Highlight mentorship, team activities, or surgical "wins" • Post aesthetic or humorous content that encourages reshares • Use hashtags like #vetmedlife, #veterinarytechnician, or #vetstudent to increase visibility	Clinic tours, staff birthday celebrations, and "Why I love working here" clips perform well.

Platform	Best for...	Use it to...	Pro Tip
TikTok	Gen Z and millennial veterinary talent, especially vet techs and recent graduates	• Show authentic, behind-the-scenes clinic culture with humor or storytelling • Create "day in the life" videos of your team members • Jump on veterinary-related trends or challenges • Educate with quick hiring tips or clinic values in under sixty seconds	Let your techs or early-career vets lead the way; they know what works here.
YouTube	Long-form storytelling, in-depth clinic showcases, or professional branding	• Post interviews with team members or leadership • Host virtual clinic tours or "Meet the Team" series • Share recorded webinars or CE-related content • Create playlists like "Working at Our Clinic" or "Vet Student Survival Tips"	YouTube is the second-largest search engine; optimize video titles and descriptions with keywords like "veterinary job San Diego" or "ER vet tech career."
Reddit and Veterinary Forums	Authentic conversations and market research	• Follow subreddits like r/Veterinary, r/VetTech, or r/VetMed and listen to what professionals are really saying • Engage subtly by answering questions, giving advice, or sharing stories • Learn about common complaints, career goals, and workplace preferences • Avoid hard selling; Reddit culture values transparency and sincerity	Think of this as "soft scouting" rather than direct outreach.
X (formerly Twitter)	Industry conversations, news, and networking with thought leaders	• Share job listings with hashtags like #vetjobs or #veterinaryhiring • Follow and engage with veterinary influencers, schools, and associations • Live-tweet from conferences or CE events • Post bite-sized insights about your clinic culture or values	Tag vet schools, professional orgs, or influencers when appropriate to increase visibility.

IMPORTANT SOCIAL MEDIA BEST PRACTICES

1. Lead With Value, Not Just Job Posts

- Avoid only posting job openings. Mix in content that educates, entertains, or inspires.

- Share tips for new graduates, career advice, CE opportunities, or industry insights.

Think: "Would I engage with this if I weren't job hunting?"

2. Be Human and Authentic

- Highlight your real team, real clinic environment, and real stories.

- Avoid overly corporate or generic language. Show your personality and values.

Behind-the-scenes snapshots, bloopers, and pet moments resonate far more than stock photos.

3. Be Consistent and Strategic

- Use a content calendar to stay consistent, even if just two to three posts per week, and post at peak times (generally lunch and evenings).

- Plan a mix of content types: video, photos, carousel posts, stories, live sessions.

Use recurring themes (e.g., "Tech Tuesday," "Mentorship Monday") to stay organized.

4. Engage With Your Audience

- Respond to comments and DMs quickly. Don't let candidates feel ignored.

- Like, comment on, or reshare others' posts in the veterinary space.

- Ask questions, run polls, or invite opinions to increase interaction.

5. Empower Your Team to Participate and Leverage Employee Networks

- Encourage team members to share your posts and tag themselves.

- Feature employees in testimonials, spotlights, or "day in the life" stories to extend reach through their networks.

- Incentivize referrals through social shares. Referrals that come through employee networks are often high-quality and a culture fit.

6. Track What Works and Replicate It

- Monitor engagement (likes, shares, DMs, link clicks) to see what resonates.

- Double down on formats and topics that get the most traction.

- Refine your approach regularly based on performance data and candidate feedback.

7. Build a Strong Employer Brand

- Share behind-the-scenes glimpses of daily life at your clinic.

- Highlight team stories, anniversaries, mentorship, or continuing education support.

- Emphasize values like work-life balance, team support, and quality medicine.

8. Engage, Don't Just Post

- Comment on vet-related posts and share insights.

- Respond to questions in vet groups and forums.

- Use polls, Q&As, and Instagram Stories to interact.

- Tag team members and encourage staff to reshare content.

9. Create Shareable, Value-Driven Content

- Tips for new graduates navigating their first job.

- Infographics about work-life balance in ER, GP, or shelter roles.

- Memes or funny/relatable veterinary technician moments.

- Case studies highlighting interesting or life-saving work.

10. Use Targeted Ads

- Run geo-targeted or interest-targeted ads for specific roles.

- Retarget visitors who've interacted with your posts or website.

- Use job title or group-based targeting on LinkedIn and Facebook.

11. Track What Works

- Use analytics to measure engagement, clicks, and conversions.

- Note which types of content generate applications or DMs.

- Double-down on high-performing formats or messages.

CHAPTER 8

Harnessing AI in Veterinary Recruiting

Every generation fears new tech. AI isn't taking over.
It's a tool, so use it wisely.

AI is transforming the veterinary recruiting landscape by streamlining processes and improving the quality of hires. For veterinary practices, where time is limited and competition for talent is fierce, AI offers powerful tools to identify, engage, and evaluate candidates more effectively. AI tools can streamline veterinary recruiting by quickly identifying qualified candidates through résumé parsing, predictive analytics, and behavioral assessments. It also enhances outreach with personalized messaging and automates routine tasks, allowing recruiters to focus on relationship-building and culture fit.

In this chapter, you will learn...

- How to use AI tools to automate résumé reviews, screening, and communication, thereby saving time and improving candidate quality

- How to use AI responsibly to reduce unconscious bias and make more equitable, data-informed hiring decisions

- The limitations of AI, including bias risks, accuracy concerns, and the importance of preserving the human touch in recruitment

- How leading ATS platforms are integrating AI to help veterinary recruiters work smarter

KEY BENEFITS OF AI IN VETERINARY RECRUITING

Artificial intelligence (AI) is transforming how veterinary practices approach recruiting, bringing new levels of speed, precision, and insight to a traditionally time-consuming and inconsistent process. By leveraging AI tools, practice owners and managers can streamline hiring, make smarter decisions, and ultimately build stronger, more resilient teams. Here are some of the most impactful ways AI is reshaping veterinary recruiting today.

Increased Efficiency

AI can rapidly sort through large volumes of applications, flagging candidates who meet predefined qualifications. This saves recruiters and practice managers hours of manual review, freeing them to focus on interviews and candidate engagement.

Improved Candidate Quality

By analyzing résumés, employment history, and other data, AI tools can help identify individuals with the right clinical skills, certifications, and experience, leading to stronger hires and better long-term fit.

Reduced Unconscious Bias

When used thoughtfully, AI can help minimize bias by focusing solely on objective criteria like skills and qualifications, supporting more equitable hiring decisions.

Faster Candidate Communication

AI-driven chatbots and email tools can answer candidate questions, provide status updates, and even schedule interviews, improving responsiveness and the overall candidate experience.

Data-Driven Recruiting Strategies

AI systems can analyze past hiring data to reveal patterns, forecast hiring needs, and optimize job postings and sourcing strategies, helping practices consistently attract better candidates.

HOW TO FIND, USE, AND MEASURE AI TOOLS IN VETERINARY RECRUITING

Understanding what AI can do is just the beginning. This section shows you how to actually put it into practice. Whether recruiting for a single clinic or managing hiring across multiple locations, here's how to explore, implement, and evaluate AI tools that can support your goals.

Step 1: Identify the Right Use Case for Your Needs

Before investing in a tool, clarify what problem you want AI to solve. Here are some common needs and the types of AI features that match.

Challenge	Solution
Need to save time reviewing applications	Look for tools with résumé parsing and automated screening capabilities.
Want to improve candidate quality	Consider platforms that offer predictive analytics or behavioral assessments to identify top traits.
Struggling to keep up with candidate communication	Use AI-powered chatbots or automated email sequencing tools that can respond quickly and schedule interviews.
Unsure of what's working	Opt for systems that include analytics dashboards so you can track sourcing performance, engagement, and conversions.

Step 2: Explore Tools Already in Your Applicant Tracking System (ATS) or Customer Relationship Management System (CRM)

You may not need to purchase a standalone AI tool. Many ATS and HR platforms now include built-in AI features such as smart candidate matching, job post optimization, automated outreach and follow-up, and diversity and bias detection.

Check with your current ATS provider to see whether AI features can be added.

Step 3: Test Standalone AI Tools for Specific Tasks

If your system lacks built-in AI or you're a smaller practice using spreadsheets or email, you can try standalone tools. Search for those with the following tools or toolkits:

- Résumé screening

- Messaging automation

- Job description optimization

- Video interview scoring

Always test with a small candidate pool first to ensure it fits your clinic's tone and hiring workflow.

Step 4: Track Effectiveness Over Time

Implementing AI isn't a "set it and forget it" decision. Track how well your tools work by monitoring time to screen or hire, candidate response rates, application-to-interview ratios, candidate quality, and retention (post-hire).

You can use these metrics to adjust filters, refine automated messages, or evaluate whether the AI's suggestions align with your clinical and cultural standards.

Step 5: Use AI to Enhance, Not Replace, Your Judgment

No matter how smart the tool, your insight into what makes a great team member is still essential. Use AI to handle the repetitive or data-heavy parts of recruiting so you can focus on building relationships with candidates, evaluating culture fit, personalizing the candidate experience, and advocating for your team's values.

Quick Recap: Matching Benefits to Tools

- Increased efficiency → Résumé parsing, candidate matching

- Improved candidate quality → Predictive analytics, skill assessments

- Reduced bias → Blind screening features, inclusive language checkers

- Faster communication → AI chatbots, automated emails

- Data-driven strategy → Dashboards, performance tracking, sourcing reports

POTENTIAL CHALLENGES TO CONSIDER

Bias in AI Algorithms

If AI tools are trained on biased or incomplete data, they may unintentionally replicate discriminatory patterns. Practices should regularly review and validate AI tools to ensure fairness.

Preserving the Human Element

While AI can automate many tasks, the human side of recruitment remains irreplaceable, such as assessing culture fit, building relationships, and supporting candidates. AI should enhance, not replace, human judgment.

Accuracy and Reliability

Veterinary professionals may question the accuracy of AI systems in understanding clinical experience or nuanced qualifications. Tools should be used as a guide and not be the final decision-maker.

Privacy and Data Security

AI systems often require access to sensitive personal information. Using trusted platforms and ensuring compliance with data privacy regulations is essential.

AI has the potential to significantly improve veterinary recruiting by increasing efficiency, reducing bias, and enabling data-driven decision-making. But technology alone isn't enough. When combined with thoughtful human oversight and ethical practices, AI becomes a powerful ally in helping veterinary practices build high-performing, compassionate teams. Many ATS platforms are adding AI capabilities to make administrative and repetitive tasks quicker and easier for the recruiter.

CHAPTER 9

The Truth About Poaching: Why It's Not Illegal (But Non-Poaching Agreements Are)

Happy employees don't leave. They become your best referrals.

In veterinary recruiting, few topics generate as much discomfort as poaching. The word often conjures images of unethical or predatory behavior, but the reality is more nuanced. Understanding the legal landscape, the role poaching plays in a competitive market, and the dangers of non-poaching agreements is essential for any practice leader who wants to attract and retain talent while staying compliant.

In this chapter, you will learn...

- Why poaching is legal and why it's a sign of a healthy, competitive job market

- How non-poaching agreements violate US antitrust laws (even if they're just a handshake or "mutual understanding")

- Non-poaching agreements' ripple effects on wages, career mobility, and employee satisfaction

- How to spot and respond to potential non-poaching arrangements.

Poaching, defined simply as recruiting someone who currently works elsewhere, is entirely legal. In fact, it's a cornerstone of a fair, competitive labor market.

However, non-poaching agreements are illegal, whether formal or informal. These are arrangements between two or more employers agreeing not to recruit or hire each other's employees. Whether sealed by a handshake, mutual understanding, or written contract, these agreements violate antitrust laws and can carry staggering legal penalties if challenged in court.

Let's break down why poaching isn't just legal but is essential for career mobility and why non-poaching agreements are both a legal hazard and a professional roadblock in veterinary medicine.

POACHING ISN'T A CRIME. IT'S A SIGNAL

Poaching implies theft, but that's a misleading metaphor. Employees are not property. They are professionals with skills, ambitions, and the right to choose their employer.

When another practice recruits your associate veterinarian or technician, they're not stealing but offering an opportunity. That opportunity is one in which your team member is free to evaluate and either accept or decline.

In fact, if your staff is being regularly recruited, it can be a compliment. It means your team is skilled, respected, and visible in the profession. It's also a healthy reminder to invest in retention, not a justification for restricting mobility or shutting down competition.

Here's the core truth: You don't "own" your employees. You earn their loyalty every day through leadership, respect, career growth opportunities, and a positive workplace culture. Poaching becomes a threat only when your retention strategy isn't strong enough to keep good people by choice.

NON-POACHING AGREEMENTS: ILLEGAL AND RISKY

In contrast, non-poaching agreements are flat-out unlawful. These arrangements, spoken or unspoken, are a form of collusion that limits competition for talent.

Under US antitrust laws, especially the Sherman Antitrust Act, any agreement between competitors not to solicit or hire each other's employees is considered a restraint of trade.

This isn't a theoretical risk. The United States Department of Justice (DOJ) and the Federal Trade Commission (FTC) have prosecuted companies for such arrangements, resulting in multi-million-dollar fines and high-profile settlements. Silicon Valley tech firms, franchise chains, and healthcare systems have all faced consequences for these practices.

There is no "safe" version of a non-poaching pact:

- A handshake agreement between two practice owners not to hire from one another is illegal.

- An email or text reading "Let's agree not to poach from each other's teams" is illegal.

- A silent understanding among local clinics not to compete for staff is illegal.

- Even refusing to interview candidates because they work for a neighboring clinic can raise legal red flags if tied to an agreement.

THE IMPACT: STIFLED CAREERS, SHRINKING OPPORTUNITIES

Non-poaching agreements don't just harm veterinary practices; they harm people. When employers agree not to compete for talent, they are…

- Blocking employees from pursuing better pay or career advancement

- Denying individuals access to specialized training or mentorship

- Forcing professionals to relocate for growth that they could have found locally

- Depressing wages across the industry by removing competitive pressure

These effects are especially damaging in veterinary medicine, where career paths are already narrow and burnout is common. In small or rural markets, a single non-poaching pact between a few practices can lock a technician or doctor into limited options unless they uproot their life entirely.

On a larger scale, non-poaching suppresses innovation, limits talent flow, and breeds stagnation. Open competition for talent challenges us to be better employers; when we rise to that challenge, the entire profession benefits.

WHAT IF YOU SUSPECT A NON-POACHING ARRANGEMENT?

If you're ever asked to honor a "gentlemen's agreement" not to recruit from certain practices, take it as a serious warning sign.

Consult legal counsel immediately if you're participating in or pressured into such an agreement. Even casual or historic agreements can expose your business to litigation or government investigation.

Whistleblowers and affected employees can bring lawsuits, and the DOJ has clarified that non-poaching enforcement is a top priority. Fines can reach tens of millions of dollars, and the reputational damage can last far longer.

The better path? Compete for talent responsibly. Build an employer brand that naturally attracts great people, and keep them engaged without closing the market to others.

A COMPETITIVE MARKET IS A HEALTHY MARKET

Yes, veterinary medicine faces a workforce shortage, but the solution isn't to circle the wagons and block outside offers. That kind of protectionism hurts everyone in the long run. Therefore, let's reframe the conversation: Poaching is not a dirty word; it's a byproduct of a market that values talent.

Your employees are not "yours." They are choosing to stay. Make that choice easy by being a workplace worth staying for, and be open to conversations if another opportunity comes their way.

Healthy competition forces us all to be better managers, mentors, leaders, and recruiters, and that's precisely the kind of competition veterinary medicine needs.

CHAPTER 10

Evaluating Résumés and CVs

*Résumés don't tell the whole story. Read between the lines.
Listen to candidates.*

Reviewing résumés may feel like a routine task, but it's one of the most consequential parts of recruiting. Within seconds, a résumé creates a first impression that can either open the door to a great hire or cause you to overlook someone with real potential. In veterinary hiring, where skill sets, certifications, and cultural fit vary widely, resumé review is both an art and a science.

This chapter gives you a practical framework for reading résumés with clarity, consistency, and confidence to quickly zero in on the best candidates and avoid common pitfalls.

In this chapter, you will learn...

- How to quickly and fairly evaluate veterinary résumés, even in high-volume situations

- The red flags and green lights to watch for in DVM and veterinary technician résumés

- How to assess clinical skills, soft skills, and growth potential from a document

- When to read between the lines and when to dig deeper

STEP 1: SCAN WITH INTENTION (THE 30-SECOND RULE)

Most recruiters or hiring managers spend less than a minute on an initial résumé review. Your first pass is about identifying whether the candidate meets your non-negotiables and shows signs of aligning with your clinic's values or needs.

Focus on...

- License or credential status, along with any specialty certifications

- Location and willingness to relocate (if needed)

- Years of relevant experience (small animal, ER, shelter, etcetera)

- Type of practice they've worked in (corporate vs. independent, GP vs. ER)

- Continuity: Do they bounce around every six to twelve months, or do they show steady growth?

Pro Tip: Keep a checklist of your clinic's baseline criteria and use it consistently when scanning résumés. This helps remove bias and speeds up the process. (AI can help with this task.)

STEP 2: EVALUATE THE CONTENT, NOT JUST THE FORMATTING

In veterinary medicine, you'll see résumés ranging from polished PDFs with personal logos to bare-bones Word docs with minimal formatting. Don't let aesthetics overly sway you; content is king.

Green lights include...

- Clear career progression or increasing responsibility

- Long-term roles or multiple years at one practice

- Mentorship experience (for DVMs) or training roles (for technicians)

- Involvement in CE, leadership, or professional organizations

- Specific mention of skills, such as dental extractions, ultrasound, fear-free handling, etcetera

Red flags include...

- Frequent job-hopping without context; context will be key in today's world

- Vague or inflated language ("seasoned veterinary leader" with one year of experience)

- Gaps in employment with no explanation

- Overly generic or templated content with no clinic names, no specific accomplishments

- Résumés that read like a job description instead of a track record

Red flags don't always mean a candidate should be ruled out, but they should trigger a deeper conversation in the phone screening or interview.

STEP 3: LOOK FOR CLINICAL AND SOFT SKILL INDICATORS

Great résumés go beyond listing duties; they reflect the candidate's impact and growth. You want to look for hints that a candidate is clinically competent but also collaborative, communicative, and adaptable.

Clinical indicators might include…

- Specific procedures performed

- Technology used

- Experience in high-volume or specialty settings

- Soft skills are often subtle, but look for…

  o Mentions of teamwork, leadership, communication, or client education

  o Involvement in staff training or mentoring

  o Community engagement or volunteer work

  o Statements of personal values or philosophy of care (especially in CVs)

DVM CVs may be longer and include publications, internships, or rotations. For new graduates, focus less on experience and more on curiosity, coachability, and clinical interests.

STEP 4: READ BETWEEN THE LINES, BUT DON'T ASSUME

Sometimes, what's missing is just as telling as what's present.

You see a résumé with...	It might suggest...	But could be the result of...
only one or two bullet points per job	underperformance	poor résumé writing
no mention of surgery or anesthesia by a technician	a skill gap	not having had the opportunity
a gap year	burnout	caregiving or an illness

Be curious, not judgmental. Always verify your assumptions during the interview. Résumés are starting points, not verdicts.

STEP 5: BUILD A REPEATABLE SCORING OR SCREENING SYSTEM

Consider using a simple scoring rubric to keep your evaluation consistent (especially across multiple roles or clinics). You might rate résumés on a 1 to 5 scale based on...

- Experience level for the role

- Relevant clinical skills

- Longevity/stability

- Communication quality (grammar, clarity, tone)

- Alignment with practice values or culture

This helps remove bias and brings structure to what can otherwise be a very subjective process.

Pro Tip: Use the résumé to inform the interview. The résumé isn't the whole story, but it tells you where to begin. Use it to...

- Ask about gaps, moves, or transitions.

- Highlight skills you want them to elaborate on.

- Confirm interest in a specific type of role or schedule.

- Identify potential mentorship or leadership qualities.

And always always personalize your outreach. Mention something you noticed in their résumé. It shows you read it and sets a collaborative tone from the start.

Evaluating résumés and CVs is more than just filtering; it's about recognizing potential, understanding nuance, and asking the right follow-up questions. As a veterinary recruiter, your job is to balance efficiency with curiosity and consistency with compassion. When done right, the résumé review becomes a screening tool and a meaningful first step in building strong veterinary teams.

ALIGN ON THE CANDIDATE'S PRIORITIES BEFORE YOU GET TO AN OFFER

A strong close starts well before the offer. During the interview process, be sure to uncover what matters most to the candidate:

- Is it schedule flexibility?

- Mentorship?

- Growth opportunities?

- A certain income floor?

- Stability and culture?

Pro Tip: Ask directly near the end of the process: "If we move toward an offer, what would a compelling opportunity look like to you?" This is so you prepare for counters from the beginning. Anticipate that top candidates may receive multiple offers. During early conversations, ask if they're interviewing elsewhere, understand what they value most in a job (compensation, schedule, culture), and clarify decision timelines and expectations. This helps you stay proactive rather than reactive.

WHY A FAST, THOUGHTFUL HIRING PROCESS MATTERS

A great hire can still go sideways without a strong onboarding experience. And onboarding doesn't start on day one; it starts when a candidate says, "I'm interested." Move candidates through your hiring process quickly and thoughtfully, from first contact to offer to their first ninety days on the job. When done well, onboarding is just the continuation of great recruiting.

It's important to streamline decision-making, get your team involved at the right stages, and keep momentum going when juggling multiple candidates simultaneously.

TIME-TO-HIRE BENCHMARKS (AND WHY SPEED REALLY MATTERS)

Let's start with a simple definition: Time-to-hire is the number of days from when a job is posted to when a candidate accepts your offer.

Across the veterinary industry, that number can vary widely depending on the role and location. For example, ER and urgent care roles often take longer to fill due to higher complexity and a smaller pool of qualified candidates.

So why does speed matter? Because in a talent-short market like veterinary medicine, the best candidates often juggle multiple offers. Every delay increases the chance of losing them or burning out the rest of your team. Longer vacancies can hurt team morale and, more importantly, patient care.

To hire top talent, you need to move faster than the practice down the street. Here are a few simple ways to tighten up your time-to-hire:

- Pre-schedule interview slots so you're not scrambling to coordinate calendars.

- Automate your screening process with questionnaires or checklists.

- Use a dashboard or applicant tracking system (ATS) to keep candidates moving smoothly through each stage.

INVOLVE THE TEAM AT THE RIGHT MOMENTS

Hiring is a team sport. But if everyone is involved too early or too late, it can slow you down or create confusion. The key is to bring the right people into the process at the right time.

Phase 1: The initial screen is done by the hiring manager, lead veterinarian, or practice administrator.

Phase 2: Introduce team members via a panel interview, working interview, or shadow shift.

Phase 3: The owner or medical director meets the candidate for a final culture alignment check.

To make this work smoothly, prep your team ahead of time.

Share the candidate's résumé and tell them what you hope to learn from the interview.

Assign interview roles. One person might focus on clinical skills, while another evaluates culture fit.

Use a shared interview rubric so everyone evaluates on the same criteria. This keeps the process fair and makes post-interview discussions more productive.

HOW TO JUGGLE MULTIPLE CANDIDATES WITHOUT DROPPING THE BALL

If you're lucky enough to have more than one great candidate in play, it can be easy to lose track of who's where in the process or, worst, accidentally ghost someone. That's where pipeline visibility becomes crucial.

Keep a clear tracker or dashboard showing where each candidate stands, and set follow-up reminders so no one slips through the cracks.

Communicate transparently: If someone's a finalist, let them know! A simple line like "You're one of three candidates we're moving forward this week" can keep engagement high without overpromising.

It's also helpful to batch similar steps together. If you're scheduling interviews, group them within the same week. And if your team needs to meet and make a decision, block time for that upfront. Don't wait until everyone's free. (Spoiler: They never will be.)

CHAPTER 11

Interviewing to Identify Fit, Not Just Skill

Skills can be taught. Culture and personality can't.

Once you've got great candidates talking to you, the next challenge is knowing who's truly right for your team. The strongest hires in veterinary medicine aren't just the ones with impressive credentials. They're the ones whose values, communication style, and personality align with your clinic culture.

In this chapter, you will learn how to…

- Design an interview process that uncovers both skill and fit so you can hire with confidence and avoid costly missteps

- Use behavioral and values-based interviewing to reveal a candidate's motivation, communication style, and alignment with your culture

- Structure a consistent interview process, from phone screens to working interviews, that helps you compare candidates fairly and objectively

- Spot red flags and green lights during interviews so you can quickly identify whether someone will thrive in your practice

- Create a two-way interview experience that shows candidates why they should choose you, while giving your team meaningful input in the decision

WHY SKILLS ALONE AREN'T ENOUGH

It's tempting to hire based on a résumé. Clinical skills, years of experience, and certifications are easy to quantify and compare. However, most hiring failures in veterinary medicine aren't about skill but fit.

Fit includes things like…

- Communication style

- Emotional intelligence

- Conflict resolution

- Coachability

- Alignment with your culture and values

A candidate can be technically strong and still be a poor addition to the team. Conversely, someone who's a little green clinically but eager to learn and a cultural match can become one of your best long-term hires. That's why smart hiring managers interview for alignment, not just ability.

The best candidates are interviewing you, too. Treat every step like a reflection of your culture. Before you begin, remember interviewing is a two-way street. Be honest. Glossing over hard truths (e.g., upcoming leadership transitions, occasional understaffing) may secure a "yes" now but lead to turnover later. For example, if your practice will be sold within the year, this must be communicated to the candidate within the rules of your possible non-disclosure agreement (NDA). People want to choose who they work for, and if a sale is underway, you will end up with very unhappy people who feel they have been misled or lied to.

Veterinary professionals have choices—lots of them. So, your interview process isn't just about evaluating them; it's also about showing candidates why they should choose you.

That means…

- Respecting their time

- Communicating clearly and promptly, even if they are not the chosen candidate

- Making them feel heard

- Creating space for real dialogue, not just a scripted Q&A

PRE-EMPLOYMENT ASSESSMENTS: BEYOND THE RÉSUMÉ

Some veterinary employers and managers use pre-employment assessments, often called behavioral, cognitive, or psychometric tests, to gain insight into a candidate's work style, problem-solving approach, and interpersonal tendencies.

These assessments aren't about labeling someone's "personality" but rather about predicting how they might perform in specific roles, fit into your team, and handle the stresses of veterinary practice. While some candidates (and employers) view them skeptically, when used thoughtfully, these tools can complement interviews and references, helping ensure you're hiring someone whose skills, temperament, and values align with your hospital's culture. It's critical to remember that assessments should never be the sole basis for a hiring decision. They're just one piece of an overall evaluation process. If you use them as a sole metric, you easily could miss out on an excellent candidate.

THE INTERVIEW PROCESS: STEP BY STEP

Step 1: Design the Interview Process Before You Start

Before you begin with your first candidate, outline a clear and consistent structure:

- Who will be involved in interviews (manager, lead tech, medical director, etcetera)?

- What interview formats will you use (phone screen, working interview, team lunch, etcetera)?

- What are you looking to evaluate at each stage?

- What questions or prompts align with your core values?

This helps eliminate bias, reduce rushed decisions, and ensure you're assessing the right things, not just who's the most charismatic.

Step 2: Start with a Phone Screen

Once a résumé passes your initial review, the next step is a quick but meaningful phone screen or a short virtual interview if you prefer video. Keeping it at fifteen to twenty minutes is excellent for the initial conversation. The goal at this stage isn't to dive deep into clinical cases or career history but to confirm the basics, understand the candidate's motivations, and set the tone for what's next. Use this time to verify key qualifications like licensure and availability, explore why they're interested in your practice or open to making a change, and give them a sense of what the rest of your hiring process looks like. Keeping it under thirty minutes helps ensure it stays focused and respectful of everyone's time, while still giving you enough information to decide whether to move forward.

Key questions to ask in a phone screen or virtual interview include...

- "What interested you in this role or our practice?"

- "What are you looking for in your next team?"

- "What have you really enjoyed or struggled with in previous roles?"

- "Is there anything you hope to avoid in your next position?"

Avoid jumping straight to compensation or logistics unless they bring it up first. Focus on fit and interest. If it's not there, don't proceed.

Step 3: Conduct a Values-Based Behavioral Interview (phone and/or virtual)

This is your main opportunity to learn who the candidate is beyond their résumé. This conversation will be more in-depth, with more details shared by both parties. This interview will continue the conversation if the initial interview uncovered the possibility of a good fit. This conversation may last longer, anywhere from thirty to forty-five minutes, depending on their conversation and desire for more details from you about the practice and the position.

Use the STAR method to gain specific, actionable insights: Situation – Task – Action – Result.

When interviewing veterinary candidates, behavioral questions guided by the STAR method help you dig beneath surface-level answers to understand how a person has handled real-world situations in the past. This method is especially helpful when assessing soft skills like communication, adaptability, ethics, and client care, traits that may not appear on a résumé but often define whether someone will thrive in your practice. Encourage candidates to walk you through the full STAR cycle with each answer.

Here's how it works:

S = Situation: Ask the candidate to describe a specific situation they encountered.

T = Task: Clarify their responsibility or goal in that scenario.

A = Action: What did they actually do? What steps did they take?

R = Result: What happened as a result? What did they learn or accomplish?

Pro Tip: If a candidate skips a step during the interview, especially the result, it's okay to prompt: "And how did that situation turn out?" or "What was the result of your actions?" This keeps the conversation focused and gives you a fuller picture of how they operate in the real world.

For quieter candidates, let them think aloud or talk through it casually. Don't rush them.

Ask follow-ups to clarify vague or overly generalized answers: "Can you walk me through that in more detail?" or "What specifically did you do in that situation?"

This structured method keeps interviews consistent, fair, and focused on real-world behavior. Over time, it also helps you compare candidates more objectively, especially when evaluating multiple people for the same role.

Look for self-awareness, ownership, and alignment, not perfect answers.

Step 4: Let Them Meet the Team

Culture fit can't be assessed in a vacuum. Meeting a candidate in person is a powerful part of the veterinary recruiting process, especially in a profession where team dynamics, emotional intelligence, and clinical presence matter just as much as technical skills. Here's why it's important and what you, as the recruiter, should pay attention to during that face-to-face time.

a. Culture Fit is Easier to Assess Live

You can observe how the candidate interacts with different team members—from reception to technicians to doctors—and how they respond to your clinic's energy, pace, and communication style. Are they warm and collaborative? Do they seem flexible or rigid? These things often don't show up on a résumé or video call.

b. You Can Gauge Emotional Intelligence and Professional Presence

Veterinary professionals work with anxious clients, injured animals, and stressed-out coworkers. Meeting someone in person gives you a clearer sense of their tone, body language, empathy, and professionalism, all of which impact client service and team morale.

c. Authenticity Tends to Shine Through

Candidates are often more relaxed and authentic in person, especially if they can see the practice, meet the team, and get a feel for their potential workspace. This leads to better conversations and more realistic expectations on both sides.

d. It's a Two-Way Street

The in-person visit is just as much about the candidate evaluating you. A strong in-clinic experience, where they feel welcomed, seen, and aligned with your values, can dramatically increase the chance they'll accept an offer.

Here's what you should observe as the candidate moves through the clinic and interacts with the team:

- Genuine interest: Do they ask thoughtful questions about your protocols, equipment, caseload, or mentorship approach?

- Communication style: Are they clear, respectful, and kind when speaking to team members at all levels?

- Adaptability: Do they seem at ease in a new environment? How do they handle unplanned interactions or distractions?

- Team engagement: When introduced to staff, do they make eye contact, smile, and show curiosity? Or do they seem passive or reserved?

- Clinical curiosity or confidence: If shadowing or observing, do they seem appropriately engaged, asking questions, noticing details, or showing eagerness to contribute?

- Energy match: Every practice has its own rhythm. Are they in sync with your practice?

Some options for in-person meetings include a team lunch or coffee with a few team members, a casual group Q&A, a panel interview, or a shadow shift or observation day, and the latter should be a paid day if they are doing more than observing. Be sure to follow state labor laws and pay candidates appropriately for their time. Even short working interviews typically require compensation.

Before the candidate arrives, coach the team on what to ask, what to consider, and how to support hiring decisions. They're not evaluating the candidate like judges but exploring chemistry, collaboration, and shared values.

Pro Tip: Encourage your team to share impressions after the visit. Technicians and CSRs often spot things you might miss, and they're the ones who will be working shoulder-to-shoulder with this person. Questions to ask your team include…

- "Did they ask good questions?"

- "Did the conversation feel natural?"

- "Do you see them fitting in with the team dynamic?"

Don't overweigh one person's opinion. Instead, look for patterns across your team's feedback. If several of your staff members report similar notes, consider that. Trust your team's instincts. If multiple people feel uneasy, dig deeper before proceeding.

Step 5: What is a Working Interview and Why Use One?

A working interview is a short, hands-on trial period where a veterinary candidate spends time in the clinic, usually a few hours to a full shift, performing aspects of the role they're applying for. Unlike a traditional interview, which focuses on conversation, a working interview allows the candidate and the team to assess real-time skills, communication style, and overall fit in the clinical environment.

Working interviews are instrumental in veterinary medicine, where technical ability, team interaction, and composure under pressure are critical. They are often used for veterinarians, technicians, and client service staff to ensure that what's on paper matches real-world performance. Working interviews can be valuable but only if they're structured and respectful. Ensure you set clear expectations, compensate candidates for their time, limit the duration, and ensure someone is guiding and checking in with the candidate. Don't use the working interview to take advantage of free labor or make a candidate work under pressure to "prove" themselves. Remember, the goal is to observe teamwork, communication, and approach.

Step 6: Questions from Candidates

Close out interviews with a statement similar to this: "We have about five minutes left. What have I failed to ask you, or what else do you feel I need to know?" Often, you can find out something important at this moment. And pay attention to what they ask; it reveals what they care about.

Great candidates often ask thoughtful questions about team dynamics, growth opportunities, leadership values, and how success is defined in the role. Other green lights to look for during interviews include honest, reflective answers, even about failures; a genuine curiosity about your culture and team; respectful communication; clear values alignment; and indications that they are teachable, team-oriented, and self-aware. These traits outperform "perfect" résumés almost every time.

At the same time, red flags to watch for during interviews include blaming language, such as "They never supported me…;" vague answers or dodging specifics, poor self-awareness or defensiveness, speaking negatively about every past role or colleague; or having no questions or curiosity about the practice.

CHAPTER 12

Making the Offer
and Closing the Deal

Details matter. Move fast, be confident, but don't push.

You've found the right candidate! Don't lose them in the final stretch. You've learned how to present a resonant offer and negotiate with transparency. Now it's time to successfully close the deal!

In this chapter, you will learn how to...

- Handle counteroffers and negotiations professionally while maintaining trust and momentum

- Structure and present an offer so it feels personal, compelling, and aligned with what the candidate values most

- Close the deal effectively, whether they say "yes" or "no," while preserving the relationship and learning for future hires

SECURING A YES!

Making a job offer is more than just a formality; it's a pivotal point in recruiting. This is where all your relationship-building, clarity, and communication come to a head. A strong close isn't just about compensation; it's about showing the candidate that you've been listening all along, understand what they value, and are prepared to deliver. In the following steps, we'll walk through exactly how to make an offer that feels personal, thoughtful, and compelling, from the first hint of a close all the way through to celebration or reflection if they say "no."

WHY OFFERS FAIL (EVEN WHEN THE INTERVIEW GOES WELL)

You've invested time, energy, and team buy-in. The candidate is a strong match. The interviews felt great. You're ready to make the offer…

…*and then they ghost you.*

Or worse, they accept a job elsewhere after "thinking about it."

This happens more often than most managers admit. It's frequently not because the candidate wasn't interested but because the offer process felt rushed, confusing, or misaligned.

In today's veterinary job market, your offer isn't a transaction; it's the beginning of a relationship.

Step 1: Make a Verbal Offer that is Personal and Clear

Don't lead with a cold email or only attach a PDF with a formal offer.

Instead, do the following:

- Call or set up a time to personally video chat with the candidate.

- Share why you're excited about them joining.

- Walk through the key elements of the offer.

- Invite questions and emphasize your flexibility and where it is, if any, e.g., benefits, hiring timeline, compensation, schedule.

Here's a sample structure:

> "We've really enjoyed getting to know you, and we think you'd be an incredible addition to our team. We'd love to extend an offer, and here's what that would look like…"

Be enthusiastic, but not pushy. Let them feel the humanness behind the opportunity.

Step 2: Put It in Writing Quickly

After the verbal conversation, follow up with a written offer letter or summary email within twenty-four hours.

It should include the following elements:

- Position title

- Start date (or proposed timeline)

- Compensation (guarantee, bonus, or base + profit share, if applicable)

- Schedule expectations (e.g., 3 x 12s, rotating weekends)

- Benefits overview (insurance, CE, PTO, licensure, etcetera)

- Reporting manager or supervisor

- Contingencies (e.g., background check)

- Reference calls and when they occur

Clarity builds trust. Ambiguity causes stalls.

Pro Tip: All offers should be in writing and contain verbiage similar to this: "All offers of employment are contingent upon the successful completion of a background screening."

Step 3: Be Ready to Negotiate Collaboratively

Negotiation doesn't mean you're being taken advantage of. It means the candidate is engaging seriously.

The following are some common requests that candidates make:

- Adjusting a shift start time

- Clarifying the bonus or incentive structure

- Adding CE or relocation support

- Increasing the starting guarantee

Instead of seeing these requests as obstacles, use them to strengthen the relationship.

Say:

> "Let's figure out what makes sense together."

> "Here's where we have flexibility, and here's where we don't."

> "This is what we've done for others in a similar position."

Approach it as a mutual problem-solving session, not a power struggle.

Step 4: Set a Clear Decision Timeline

Open-ended offers kill momentum. Give them a window to decide, but be sure to respect the time they need to make a decision as important as this one. Consider using this sample script:

> "Take a few days to think it over. Would it feel fair to circle back by Friday?"

This gives structure without pressure. Communicate that you will be available for questions during this time frame.

Step 5: Handle Counters or Hesitations Professionally

You should be prepared as if you have been preparing for counters from the beginning. Reiterate that you understand what they value most in a job (compensation, schedule, culture), and clarify decision timelines and expectations. This helps you stay proactive rather than reactive.

When a candidate hesitates or presents a counter, don't take it personally or rush to match it. Stay calm and curious, and ask open-ended questions:

- "What's important to you about an offer?"

- "What would make you feel confident choosing us?"

This opens dialogue and reveals motivators behind their hesitation.

Additionally, create room for flexibility without panic. You can respond to a counter like this:

> "Let me take this back to the team and see what we can do. We really value you and want this to be a great fit for both sides."

If the counter is outside your compensation structure, emphasize intangibles that align with their long-term goals. Reframe the value, and remind them of the full value proposition:

- Culture

- Mentorship (especially for newer graduates)

- Medical autonomy

- Growth opportunities

- Stability (e.g., privately owned vs. corporate)

This shows a willingness to collaborate without weakening your position.

However, sometimes a candidate will not budge on a compensation request or may seem hesitant based on fear or over-analysis. In these scenarios, remember that it's okay to maintain set boundaries and walk away.

Say something like "We want someone who's genuinely excited to join us, not someone who feels torn. We support your decision either way."

Sometimes, letting go is the power move.

Step 6: If They Say "Yes," Celebrate Immediately

Don't wait for onboarding to show a candidate they made the right choice.

Do the following within twenty-four hours of the "yes:"

- Send a welcome email or e-card.

- Snail mail is still appreciated!

- Announce the hire internally.

- Assign a team buddy or mentor to the new hire.

- Share what's next (e.g., credentialing, onboarding schedule, etcetera).

Even a simple message like *"We're so excited you're joining us; you made our week!"* goes a long way in reinforcing the relationship.

Step 7: If They Say "No," Ask Why and Learn

Not every offer will close. That's okay. But don't let a "no" be a dead end.

Respectfully ask, *"If you're comfortable sharing, was there anything we could have done differently, or was there something in particular that influenced your decision?"*

This allows the candidate to share honest insights that can help improve your practice's future offers, and sometimes the door stays open for later.

DECISION-MAKING FRAMEWORKS FOR MAKING OFFERS

A weighted scoring system can be effective during hiring decisions because it helps you evaluate candidates more objectively, consistently, and strategically. For example, clinical skill and communication each account for thirty percent of the decision, while adaptability and culture fit each account for twenty percent of the decision. Compare apples to apples by standardizing interview questions and feedback forms.

When in doubt, go back to your hiring goals. For example, is this person some-one you want on a tough overnight with limited help? Can you see them leading or mentoring in six to twelve months? If they fit your goals, they're likely a good candidate.

Red Flags During Offer Negotiations

- Ghosting or long delays without updates

- Significant last-minute changes in expectations

- Pressure for things far outside your compensation framework

- Disrespectful or transactional tone

Don't force the fit if someone is showing significant signs of misalignment. How they handle the offer tells you how they'll handle future decisions.

Green Lights During Offer Negotiations

- Prompt responses and thoughtful questions

- Transparency about personal goals or concerns

- Requests that are reasonable and values-based

- Gratitude and genuine excitement

These are the signals of a good-faith candidate who's likely to stick around.

Don't let perfection delay action: An eighty-five percent match who's coachable is often better than a ninety-five percent match who appears unwilling to learn.

CHAPTER 13

Veterinary Employment Offers and Contracts— What to Include and Why

Contracts protect everyone. Review them with an attorney.

Having a clear, well-constructed employment contract is essential when you've found your ideal veterinary candidate and are ready to make an offer. This document formalizes the relationship and protects both the practice and the new hire by clearly setting expectations from day one.

In this chapter, you will learn how to...

- Understand the key differences between an offer of employment and a full employment contract and when to use each

- Identify the must-have clauses that protect both the practice and the veterinarian

- Avoid common pitfalls that can lead to misunderstandings, disputes, or turnover

- Use contracts strategically to support retention, compliance, and smooth onboarding

WHY EMPLOYMENT CONTRACTS MATTER

A veterinary employment contract is more than a formality; it's a legal safeguard and a tool for clarity. It prevents misunderstandings, ensures both parties know their responsibilities, and can serve as a retention strategy by outlining incentives and career growth opportunities. A strong contract also lays the foundation for a smooth onboarding process, helping new hires integrate successfully from day one.

Consider these scenarios:

- A new associate veterinarian joins without a contract, only to learn later that weekend ER coverage is expected twice a month, something never discussed during hiring. This misunderstanding causes tension and, ultimately, early resignation.

- A technician signs on with a practice offering a CE allowance, but the contract doesn't specify that unused funds don't carry over. The employee assumes they can roll it into the following year, leading to frustration when told otherwise.

These situations highlight how easily minor oversights can lead to dissatisfaction, turnover, or even legal disputes.

OFFERS OF EMPLOYMENT VS. EMPLOYMENT CONTRACTS

An offer of employment is a short, straightforward document outlining the basic terms you're extending to a candidate. It can…

- Confirm the candidate's interest before drafting a full contract

- Summarize essentials like position, salary, start date, and benefits

- Keep the hiring process moving quickly in competitive markets

- An offer letter is generally not legally binding in the same way as a contract is. Consider it an invitation or a written handshake that may lead to negotiations.

An employment contract, in contrast, is…

- Legally binding once signed

- Far more detailed, covering legal clauses, termination policies, restrictive covenants, and dispute resolution

- Designed to protect both the employer and the employee in the long term

A best practice is to issue an offer letter to secure agreement on high-level terms and begin pre-boarding. Follow up with a full employment contract before the start date, allowing the candidate time to review and, if desired, consult legal counsel.

Every contract should be tailored to the role and jurisdiction, but most will include:

Job Title and Duties

Outline the scope of work clearly, including clinical responsibilities, leadership roles, on-call requirements, and any community outreach expectations. Avoid vague phrasing like "other duties as assigned" without context.

Compensation and Benefits

Specify base salary, bonus structures, production models, profit-sharing arrangements, and benefits such as PTO, insurance, retirement plans, CE allowances, and signing or relocation bonuses. Be clear on timelines, e.g., when bonuses are calculated or CE funds become available.

Work Schedule and Hours

Define regular hours, shift patterns, weekend or emergency coverage expectations, and overtime or compensatory time off policies.

Term of Employment and Termination

State whether the role is at-will or for a fixed term. Detail notice periods for resignation or termination and outline severance, if any.

Restrictive Covenants

Non-compete clauses should be reasonable in scope, duration, and geography. Many candidates are pushing back against non-compete clauses, and many states are outlawing them. Check with your state and local rules. Non-solicitation clauses protect against poaching clients.

Confidentiality

Address the protection of client information, patient records, and proprietary business processes.

Professional Development and Licensing

Clarify licensing requirements, continuing education obligations, and who covers associated costs.

Dispute Resolution

Outline whether disputes will go through mediation, arbitration, or litigation, and in what jurisdiction.

NEGOTIATING EMPLOYMENT CONTRACTS

Many veterinary professionals, especially new graduates, have never negotiated a contract. As an employer, you set the tone. Transparency and fairness during this stage not only increase acceptance rates but also foster goodwill that carries into the working relationship.

Tips for Smooth Negotiations

- Be upfront about non-negotiable terms early in the process.

- Listen to the candidate's concerns and explore compromises where possible.

- Explain the reasoning behind clauses, especially restrictive covenants.

- Document changes to ensure both sides have the same understanding before signing.

Common mistakes to avoid include using generic templates without tailoring them to veterinary practice realities; skipping legal review, especially for multi-state or remote roles; failing to address compensation timing, such as production payouts or CE reimbursements; and overly broad non-compete clauses that may not hold up in court and that may scare off strong candidates.

CONTRACTS AS A RETENTION TOOL

A contract that clearly spells out growth pathways, CE support, and performance bonuses is more than a legal document; it's a commitment to the employee's future in your practice. This sends a message: We want you here long-term, and we're investing in you.

Employees who feel valued and protected are far more likely to remain with the practice, reducing costly turnover and preserving team morale.

Bottom line: An offer letter gets the ball rolling, but the real commitment happens in the employment contract. By using strategic planning and drafting contracts with clarity, fairness, and legal precision, veterinary practices can hire faster, protect their interests, and build lasting, productive relationships with their teams.

CHAPTER 14

Onboarding That Builds Retention

Have a plan. Work the plan. Check in often.

A great hire can still go sideways without a strong onboarding experience. This chapter explores how to design the first week and the first ninety days that build connection, confidence, and long-term loyalty. Onboarding is simply a continuation of recruitment.

In this chapter, you will learn...

- What to do and what to avoid in the first ninety days

- How to set up clinical mentorship or buddy systems

- How to integrate new hires into team culture

- Checklists, timelines, and onboarding playbooks

WHY THE FIRST NINETY DAYS MATTER

The first ninety days of a new hire's journey are pivotal. In veterinary medicine, where stress is high, the steep learning curve, and team dynamics are everything, those first few weeks can cement loyalty or plant seeds of doubt. Research across industries shows that many employees decide within their first three months whether to stay for the long haul. In vet med, poor onboarding is one of the top contributors to early turnover.

That's why it's not enough to just "show them around" and hope they figure it out. A structured, supportive onboarding plan makes all the difference for performance, retention, and morale.

WHAT TO DO DURING THE FIRST NINETY DAYS

Day One: Make It Welcoming, Not Overwhelming

Your goal is to build connection, not throw them into chaos. A warm, well-orchestrated day one sets the tone.

- Greet them warmly; have someone waiting when they arrive.

- Set up all tech access in advance (email, software logins).

- Schedule a team lunch or coffee to foster connection.

- Avoid assigning clients or solo duties on day one.

- Complete federal/state paperwork and HR forms if they have not already been done.

Weeks One through Four: Structure, Support, and Clarity

This is the time to orient your new hire without overwhelming them. Shadowing and feedback should be frequent.

- Provide a structured shadowing schedule across different roles.

- Be clear about expectations and responsibilities.

- Hold regular check-ins either daily or every other day is ideal.

Weeks Five through Twelve: Build Autonomy Gradually

- As their confidence grows, so should their independence. But don't disappear too soon. Allow for increasing levels of clinical autonomy.

- Hold weekly coaching sessions with their mentor or supervisor.

- Schedule at least one formal feedback conversation before the end of ninety days.

WHAT TO AVOID

Even well-intentioned teams can accidentally create stress or confusion for new hires. Avoid these common onboarding pitfalls:

- Throwing them into the fire: Starting with emergencies or full appointments without support sends the wrong message.

- Overloading with policies: Don't hand them a thirty-page handbook without explanation. Context matters.

- Assuming they'll "just fit in:" Culture integration doesn't happen passively; it requires intentional effort from leadership and the team.

SETTING UP CLINICAL MENTORSHIP OR BUDDY SYSTEMS

One of the most effective onboarding strategies is pairing new hires with a mentor or buddy. These roles are different but complementary. Avoid assigning burned-out or disengaged team members as mentors, and make sure the mentor genuinely wants to mentor because forced pairings often backfire.

Buddy = A peer-level support person who helps with day-to-day logistics, workflow questions, and team dynamics.

Mentor = A senior veterinarian who provides clinical coaching, reviews cases, and supports professional development.

How to Structure for Success

- Schedule weekly thirty-minute mentor check-ins for the first eight to twelve weeks.

- Encourage co-managing cases during the first few shifts.

- Set and review clinical development milestones, such as first solo surgery or overnight shift autonomy.

INTEGRATING NEW HIRES INTO TEAM CULTURE

Culture fit doesn't have to be a mystery; it can (and should) be intentionally nurtured.

- Introduce them with a few personal facts or fun trivia at a team meeting.

- Plan a first-shift potluck, coffee run, or give a small welcome gift bag.

- Use rotating "culture check" roles. Ask different team members to name one positive thing the new hire did on each shift.

- Help them feel included by inviting them to team outings, group CE events, or wellness sessions early on. And don't just ask how they're performing; ask how they're feeling.

Watch for signs of isolation, such as always eating lunch alone, quietness during rounds or downtime, being hesitant to ask for help, or being unclear on workflows. These signs may indicate they're struggling to connect, and it's your cue to intervene supportively.

USE CHECKLISTS, TIMELINES, AND ONBOARDING PLAYBOOKS

A written onboarding plan saves time, improves consistency, and prevents steps from falling through the cracks. Create an onboarding playbook that includes…

- Logistics: payroll setup, benefits info, and software systems

- Clinical systems: SOAP standards, anesthesia protocols, and pharmacy access

- Culture: conflict resolution, communication norms, and gratitude rituals

- Build in Role-Specific Milestones for 30/60/90 Days

- First solo shift or procedure

- Introduction to key protocols or workflows

- Scheduled performance check-ins and feedback loops

USE A DIGITAL OR PHYSICAL CHECKLIST FOR KEY TASKS

- Equipment issued and passwords set

- Introductions to all team members

- Shadowed X number of procedures or cases

- First performance review scheduled

When done right, onboarding isn't just orientation; it's retention in action. The time and thought you invest now will pay off in long-term engagement, clinical growth, and team loyalty.

CHAPTER 15

Building a Long-Term Talent Strategy

Hire for today. Plan for tomorrow.

Most veterinary practices consider hiring a reaction to an empty role, but the strongest teams are built with foresight, not urgency. A long-term talent strategy ensures you're attracting great candidates today and creating systems that sustain recruiting success for years to come.

In this chapter, you will learn…

- How to make recruiting intentional, measurable, and sustainable

- Why building a diverse team is not only ethical but a strategic advantage that improves culture, communication, and resilience

- Practical steps to audit your hiring practices, write inclusive job postings, and expand candidate sourcing beyond traditional channels

- How to create a welcoming onboarding experience and workplace culture that retains diverse talent

- The importance of tracking key performance indicators (KPIs) to understand your hiring effectiveness and make data-driven improvements

- How to build and use simple dashboards and scorecards to keep leadership informed and ensure continuous recruiting success

Great hiring isn't just about filling today's role. It's about building an infrastructure that draws top talent to you, year after year.

BUILDING A DIVERSE TEAM INTENTIONALLY

A diverse team isn't just a nice-to-have; it's a strategic advantage. Diverse teams bring broader perspectives, improve client communication, and create stronger, more resilient workplace cultures. But meaningful diversity doesn't happen by chance. It requires intentional recruitment practices that look beyond the usual channels and challenge unexamined biases. This means writing inclusive job postings, actively sourcing candidates from underrepresented groups, and fostering an environment where every team member feels welcome and valued. Your leadership sets the tone. When you commit to building a team that reflects the community you serve, you help shape a more equitable and forward-thinking veterinary profession.

AUDIT YOUR CURRENT TEAM AND HIRING PRACTICES

Start by taking an honest look at your current team makeup. Are there gaps in representation? Do your job postings, interview panels, or outreach methods unintentionally limit your candidate pool? Identify where bias—conscious or unconscious—may exist in your processes.

WRITE INCLUSIVE JOB DESCRIPTIONS

Use clear, gender-neutral language. Avoid jargon or qualifications that aren't truly essential. For example, don't include "must have 5+ years in a high-volume ER" if you're open to training. Consider adding a diversity or inclusion statement to show your commitment. Don't just market your practice as diverse as a marketing ploy; be sincere in creating a diverse team.

EXPAND WHERE YOU SOURCE CANDIDATES

Move beyond the usual job boards. Connect with veterinary associations that serve underrepresented groups, historically Black colleges and universities (HBCUs), and community-based programs. Engage with local high schools or community colleges to grow a pipeline of future diverse talent. There are many diversity-veterinary-specific groups available now on social media platforms.

STANDARDIZE YOUR INTERVIEW PROCESS

Use structured interviews with consistent questions for all candidates to reduce bias. Include diverse voices on interview panels when possible. Focus on competencies and potential, not just "fit."

CREATE AN INCLUSIVE ONBOARDING AND WORK CULTURE

A diverse hire won't stay long in an exclusive environment. Foster a culture where team members feel safe speaking up, sharing ideas, and being themselves. Offer mentorship, celebrate different backgrounds, and address microaggressions or inequities head-on.

TRACKING AND ADJUSTING YOUR TALENT STRATEGY: KPIs AND METRICS

Metrics matter because veterinary recruiting is too critical and too costly to leave up to gut feeling alone. Whether you're a full-time recruiter, a practice owner, or a manager wearing multiple hats, tracking your recruiting metrics gives you clarity, control, and confidence. When you measure what matters, you can improve what matters.

Tracking progress allows you to spot what's working and double down, catch issues early before positions sit open for months, improve the candidate experience based on real data, and confidently communicate your value to leadership.

WHAT KPIs SHOULD YOU TRACK?

Not all metrics are helpful, and not every clinic needs the same key performance indicators (KPIs). The right ones for your practice will depend on your goals, hiring volume, and roles you're filling. Here are the core KPIs most veterinary recruiters should consider and why they matter:

KPI	Why It Matters
Time-to-fill	Shows how quickly roles are being filled from job post to offer acceptance. Long delays may mean unrealistic expectations or bottlenecks
Time-to-start	Measures how long it takes from offer acceptance to the first day. Delays can lead to lost candidates or gaps in care
Offer acceptance rate	High offer rejection could signal issues with compensation, reputation, or the interview process
Source of hire	Helps you invest in the right platforms (e.g., referrals vs. job boards vs. social media outreach)
Retention at ninety days	A strong indicator of onboarding effectiveness and cultural alignment
Interview-to-offer ratio	Reveals how many interviews it takes to make a hire where a high number may signal poor screening or misaligned expectations
Cost-per-hire (optional but helpful)	Helps you track ROI if you're spending on ads, recruiters, or platforms

WHAT IF YOUR KPIs AREN'T WHERE YOU WANT THEM?

Missed goals aren't failure; they're feedback. Here's how to respond when the numbers don't meet expectations.

If...	Then...
Time-to-fill is too long	Audit your job post for clarity and appeal. Speed up scheduling. Shorten your process. Build a pipeline.
Offer acceptance rate is low	Ask candidates for feedback. Review and improve your offer package. Be transparent earlier.
If ninety-day retention is poor	Revisit onboarding and mentorship plans. Conduct exit or stay interviews. Assign cultural ambassadors.

CREATING A VETERINARY RECRUITING DASHBOARD

You don't need fancy software to create a veterinary recruiting dashboard. Use Google Sheets, Excel, or basic recruiting tools to track and color-coding and reminders to highlight wins and issues.

What to Track	How to Track It
Open roles	Job title, date posted, current status, and the hiring stage
Pipeline Status	Number of applicants, interviews, offers, declines
Time Metrics	Average time-to-fill, interview to offer time
Source Metrics	Applicants and hires by source
Candidate Experience	Interview feedback, follow-up timelines
Retention Snapshots	30/60/90-day retention checks

Use this dashboard to build a monthly scorecard, a simple summary to share with leadership showing your recruiting activity, successes, and areas to improve.

FINAL THOUGHTS

Tracking your recruiting efforts isn't busywork; it's building a more innovative, repeatable process that saves time and leads to stronger hires. The best recruiters don't just fill roles; they create systems that start with tracking what matters.

CHAPTER 16

Managing Turnover and Exit Interviews

Don't cling to expired talent. Let them go, and learn as they leave.

Turnover is inevitable in veterinary medicine, but it doesn't have to catch you off guard. Every resignation is a chance to gain insight into what's working, what's not, and what you can do better moving forward. Rather than reacting with frustration or blame, take a strategic approach to understanding and addressing the root causes behind team departures. That process starts with conducting structured, thoughtful exit interviews.

In this chapter, you will learn...

- How to conduct meaningful exit interviews that provide actionable insights for improving your practice

- Effective strategies to prevent burnout and create a culture that promotes long-term retention

- Practical ways to build belonging and engagement so team members feel valued and invested

- How to document, analyze, and act on feedback to reduce turnover and strengthen your workplace culture

CONDUCTING EXIT INTERVIEWS THAT LEAD TO REAL CHANGE

Exit interviews can be a goldmine of insight if they're handled correctly. But too often, they're rushed, optional, or ignored entirely. To turn feedback into action, consistency is key.

Here's how to make exit interviews meaningful:

- Use a standard exit interview form or digital survey to keep employee feedback organized and comparable.

- Identify trends quarterly, especially if multiple team members mention similar themes (e.g., lack of mentorship, high caseloads, or management disconnect).

- Share findings in leadership meetings and treat them as data, not personal criticism. The goal isn't to dwell on the past but to improve the future.

PREVENTING BURNOUT AND IMPROVING RETENTION

In most practices, burnout isn't a buzzword; it's a reality. And it's one of the leading causes of voluntary turnover in veterinary teams. Burnout doesn't always look like exhaustion. Sometimes, it looks like disengagement, irritability, or a once-motivated team member quietly pulling away.

Contrary to popular belief, burnout isn't just about working too many hours. It's a chronic imbalance between demands and resources, and it's made worse when team members feel unappreciated, micromanaged, or unheard.

Burnout Prevention Strategies That Actually Work

- Conduct anonymous "pulse checks" on team well-being at least quarterly

Build structured time off into schedules, including occasional mental health days

- Respect caseload boundaries, especially on ER, surgery, or overnight shifts

- Normalize access to support: peer debriefs after tough cases, therapy stipends, or access to professional coaching

BUILDING BELONGING: THE KEY TO LONG-TERM RETENTION

Pay and workload matter, but belonging is often the deciding factor between a teammate staying or leaving. People want to feel seen, valued, and part of something bigger than themselves.

Practical Ways to Build Belonging

- Celebrate personal and professional milestones, such as birthdays, certifications, and work anniversaries.

- Give team members a say in protocols, workflows, or changes that impact their daily work.

- Offer growth without pressure: provide CE stipends, create mentorship or teaching tracks, and make leadership roles available, but optional.

RE-RECRUIT YOUR TEAM BEFORE SOMEONE ELSE DOES

Retention isn't a one-time achievement; it's ongoing. One of the most powerful strategies you can use is regularly re-recruiting your team. This means checking in with the same curiosity and care you use with job candidates.

Ask each team member periodically, "If you were offered the job again today, would you say 'yes'?" If the answer is anything less than an enthusiastic yes, don't panic. Ask why. Listen fully. And take action before they start job searching.

When managing turnover, the goal isn't zero departures: It's healthy, informed departures with minimal regret and maximum learning. When you pair exit interviews with proactive burnout prevention and a strong culture of belonging, you'll retain your best people and earn their loyalty for the long haul.

Let your team know they can come to you with information about employers or recruiters reaching out to them to discuss.

HOW TO DOCUMENT AND UTILIZE FEEDBACK

Collecting feedback is only the first step. How you document, share, and act on it truly matters. Without a straightforward process, even the most valuable insights get buried in email threads or forgotten after a busy week. When handled well, feedback becomes a powerful tool for improving retention, morale, and recruiting outcomes.

Step 1: Choose a Consistent Format

Create a central place to store all feedback, ideally digital, searchable, and accessible to leadership. This could be as simple as a shared Google Drive folder or a more structured HR tool.

For each piece of feedback, record the following:

- Date received

- Source (exit interview, anonymous survey, one-on-one, etcetera)

- Topic area (e.g., workload, leadership, communication, pay, culture)

- Summary of what was said

- Action status (logged, under review, in progress, resolved)

- Use tags or categories so you can identify patterns over time (e.g., "mentorship concerns" or "workflow delays")

Step 2: Identify Themes and Trends

One comment might be an outlier, but if multiple people raise the same concern, that's a trend worth addressing. Review all feedback monthly or quarterly to identify:

- Recurring issues (e.g., lack of training support, unclear protocols, feeling undervalued)

- Team-specific concerns (Is this isolated to techs? DVMs? a single shift?)

- Positive themes (What's going well that you can amplify?)

Use simple dashboards or spreadsheets to track these trends over time. Visual tools like bar charts or word clouds can be surprisingly helpful in team meetings.

Step 3: Share Insights With Leadership

Don't keep feedback in a vacuum. Set aside time in monthly leadership or staff meetings to share anonymized insights, especially if any of the following are true:

- Multiple people have raised the same issue

- A change has been implemented, and feedback shows whether it's working or not

- You want to highlight a positive cultural shift or win

- Keep the tone solution-oriented: the goal is not blame; it's progress.

Step 4: Take Visible, Actionable Steps

When people give feedback and see no change, trust erodes quickly. Even minor improvements can make a big difference if visible and acknowledged. Close the loop with a statement: "We heard from several team members that XYZ was frustrating, so we're trying ABC this month." Pilot ideas before a full rollout by inviting the team into the process. And give credit; let the team know their voices helped spark change.

Step 5: Build a Feedback Culture

When feedback becomes part of the regular rhythm, not just during exits, it helps create a workplace where people feel heard, respected, and invested. Ways to normalize feedback include...

- Regular "stay interviews" or casual check-ins

- Anonymous pulse surveys

- A suggestion box—digital or physical—with a regular review process

- Public wins board where you share what's been improved thanks to team input

Documented feedback isn't just recordkeeping; it's a roadmap. When you take it seriously and respond with action, you build a stronger team, reduce avoidable turnover, and position your practice as a place where people want to stay and grow.

Remember, every departure is a chance to improve your clinic. If you treat turnover like feedback, not failure, you'll build a stronger, more resilient team for the long haul.

CHAPTER 17

The Veterinary Recruiter Job Description

Recruiters aren't "extra." They're essential.
Define the role, then let them do their job.

Hiring doesn't happen by accident; it happens because someone is dedicated to making it work. In many veterinary practices, that responsibility falls to a manager, administrator, or an internal recruiter who wears many hats. The role of the veterinary recruiter is more than just posting jobs and scheduling interviews; it's about building relationships, shaping the team, and ensuring the practice has the right people to deliver excellent care. Whether it's a standalone role or part of your broader responsibilities, understanding the core functions of recruiting is essential to long-term success.

In this chapter, you will learn...

- The core responsibilities and daily tasks of a veterinary recruiter

- How recruiting fits into veterinary practice management and reporting lines

- Key qualifications and skills needed for success in this role

- Tips for attracting and engaging top veterinary talent effectively

JOB DESCRIPTION

A veterinary recruiter or veterinary talent acquisition manager within a veterinary practice plays a crucial role in identifying, attracting, and hiring qualified professionals to meet the practice's staffing needs. Here's a typical job description:

Job Title: Veterinary Recruiter

This role may fall under your responsibilities as a manager or administrator, and you typically report to the practice owner or medical director. As a manager or administrator, you should view recruiting as a core part of your job, not a distraction. If you are an internal recruiter, you may report to the practice manager, administrator, operations director, or practice owner.

Job Summary: The veterinary recruiter manages the full-cycle recruitment process for veterinary professionals, including veterinarians, veterinary technicians, and support team members. This role ensures the practice attracts top-tier talent that aligns with our mission, culture, and service standards. The ideal candidate is proactive, personable, and knowledgeable about the veterinary industry.

Key Responsibility	Description
Staffing Strategy	Partner with leadership to assess staffing needs and define role requirements
Job Advertising	Create and post engaging job ads on various platforms
Candidate Sourcing	Actively source candidates via databases, social media, networking, and outreach campaigns
Screening and Interviews	Screen résumés and conduct initial interviews for qualifications and culture fit
Interview Coordination	Schedule and manage interviews between candidates and hiring managers
Candidate Experience	Manage the entire process from application to offer and onboarding
Recruitment Tracking	Maintain recruitment pipeline via an applicant tracking system (ATS) or spreadsheet
Relationship Building	Engage with veterinary schools, internship programs, and industry organizations
Industry Awareness	Stay current on hiring trends, compensation benchmarks, and workforce challenges
Employer Branding	Promote the practice's culture through events, content, and online presence

QUALIFICATIONS

Requirement Type	Details
Experience	2+ years in recruiting (veterinary or healthcare preferred)
Knowledge	Familiarity with veterinary roles, titles, licensing, and trends
Skills	Excellent communication, organizational, and interpersonal skills. Understanding/ knowledge of veterinary terminology
Tech Proficiency	Experience with ATS and recruiting tools
Soft Skills	Strong discretion, professionalism, and ability to work independently as well as a sales mindset

PREFERRED EDUCATION

Degrees: bachelor's in HR, business, communications, or a related field

Certifications: Society for Human Resource Management (SHRM) (various levels), Certified Professional Veterinary Recruiter (CPVR), Professional Veterinary Recruiter (PVR), Certified Internet Recruiter (CIR), Certified Diversity Recruiter (CDR), Human Resources Certification Institute (HRCI)

CHAPTER 18

Internal vs. External Veterinary Recruiters

Internal recruiters need space to focus. External recruiters? Treat them like the trusted advisors they are.

Veterinary recruiting is both an art and a science, and choosing the right person or partner to lead your hiring efforts can significantly impact your practice's success. In most practices, recruitment is managed internally by a practice manager, medical director, or administrator, depending on the roles needed. However, as the hiring landscape becomes more competitive and complex, partnering with an external veterinary recruiter deserves your serious consideration.

Let's explore the key differences between internal and external recruiters, how to evaluate your in-house capabilities, and when it makes sense to bring in outside recruiting support.

In this chapter, you will learn...

- The key differences between internal and external veterinary recruiters, including the pros and cons of each

- The various external recruiting models and when to consider each one for your practice

- How to evaluate, choose, and build a successful partnership with an external veterinary recruiter

- Tips for integrating internal and external recruiting efforts to maximize hiring success

UNDERSTANDING INTERNAL RECRUITING

Internal recruiting refers to talent acquisition managed by yourself or someone already on your team. This may include...

- A practice manager or hospital administrator

- A medical director (especially for clinical positions)

- A dedicated internal recruiter (in larger organizations)

Pros of Internal Recruiting	
Deep cultural insight	Internal team members should have an intimate understanding of your values, pace, personalities, and what makes someone a great fit.
Cost-effective	There are no third-party fees involved.
Greater control	You can directly manage priorities, messaging, and candidate engagement.

Cons of Internal Recruiting	
Limited reach	Internal teams may lack access to national databases or passive candidates.
Time constraints	Recruiting is often just one of many responsibilities, leading to inconsistent or delayed efforts.
Resource gaps	Internal recruiters may not have access to robust sourcing tools, employer branding strategies, or the time to run a full-scale search.

UNDERSTANDING EXTERNAL VETERINARY RECRUITERS

External recruiters are third-party professionals or agencies hired to identify (source), attract, and pre-screen candidates for your open positions. Depending on skills, they may conduct an in-depth interview as well. They may work under contingency, retained, flat fee, or subscription models, and ideally, they specialize in veterinary medicine.

Pros of External Recruiting	
Access to wider talent pools	They can reach passive candidates, employed veterinarians, and national databases.
Speed and efficiency	With recruiting as their full-time focus, external partners can often move faster.
Market insights	They offer real-time knowledge of compensation trends, candidate expectations, and talent availability.
Discretion	If you're replacing a current employee or conducting a confidential search, external partners can work quietly and professionally.

Cons of External Recruiting	
Variable quality	Not all recruiters are equal; some may lack veterinary expertise or alignment with your practice's needs.
Cultural disconnect	Even experienced recruiters won't know your team as intimately unless you invest in the relationship.

TYPES OF EXTERNAL VETERINARY RECRUITING MODELS

As you consider external help, it's important to understand the different models that recruiters use and their strengths and drawbacks.

Recruiting Model	How it works	Pros	Cons	Best for...
Contingency Recruiters	Contingency recruiters are only paid if they successfully place a candidate. Some may charge a retainer upfront, which is deducted from the final placement fee and is typically a percentage of the candidate's first-year base salary (not total compensation, unless otherwise specified).	• No payment unless a placement is made • Recruiters are motivated to move quickly • You can usually work with multiple recruiters simultaneously and often continue to search on your own as well	• Can be volume-focused rather than quality-focused • May push candidates who aren't long-term fits • Risk of recruiters prioritizing speed over alignment	Urgent, hard-to-fill roles; practices open to working with multiple agencies
Flat Fee Recruiters	You pay a fixed fee for the service, regardless of the candidate's salary or time to hire. Payments can vary and may be upfront, partially upfront, or due upon placement.	• Predictable budgeting • Often more collaborative than contingency models • May include additional services depending on experience of recruiter and include consulting services	• You typically will pay a fee regardless of the hiring outcome • Less incentive to fill the role quickly or find the perfect fit • Not ideal for multiple roles unless bundled	Practices with set budgets and clear hiring plans; non-urgent positions

Recruiting Model	How it works	Pros	Cons	Best for...
Subscription-Based Recruiters	You pay a monthly fee for ongoing recruiting support. This may include a set number of hires per month, unlimited hiring within a time period, or access to a dedicated recruiter. It may not include actual placements because the focus is on introductions more than one-off placements.	• Ideal for practices with consistent or high-volume hiring needs • Encourages deeper familiarity with your practice culture • Costs are spread out over time	• You pay, even if you make no hires that month • Requires a longer-term commitment and planning • Less practical for one-off roles	Growing or multi-location veterinary groups with regular recruiting needs.
Exclusive Veterinary Recruiting Agreements	An exclusive agreement gives a single recruiter or firm the sole right to fill a position during a set period. This can apply to any recruiter model (contingency, flat fee, or subscription). During this exclusivity window, no other recruiters or internal teams may source candidates for that role. Some contracts also require payment for any hire made during the exclusive period, even if the candidate comes from your own efforts.	• Greater investment from the recruiter • Stronger partnership and collaboration • Avoids candidate ownership disputes • One consistent voice representing your practice	• Risk if the recruiter underdelivers • No competitive pressure to perform • You're limited to one sourcing channel for the role	Confidential, high-level, or mission-critical roles (e.g., medical director, lead DVM); practices seeking a deeper partnership

If you happen to be the one seeking a new position, these same insights will help you choose and work with a veterinary recruiter who's the right fit for your ongoing veterinary career journey.

Pro Tip: Success with exclusive agreements depends on choosing the right recruiter, someone with a veterinary track record, a strong network, and a collaborative mindset.

WHEN TO USE AN EXTERNAL VETERINARY RECRUITER

Think of external recruiters as you do your other professional advisors: accountants, lawyers, and marketing experts. Bringing in a recruiter can be a strategic business decision in the following situations:

- Your internal efforts have stalled.

- The job's been posted for weeks (or months) with no qualified applicants.

- You're hiring for a highly specialized or hard-to-fill role.

- You need to hire discreetly.

- You need to conduct a confidential search without alerting your current team or community.

- You're opening a new location or expanding services.

- Scaling requires more recruiting bandwidth than internal teams may have.

- You simply don't have the time.

- Recruiting becomes a full-time job and may compete with patient care or operations.

- You're not seeing quality candidates.

A recruiter can elevate your search and present stronger, better-aligned talent.

HOW TO WORK EFFECTIVELY WITH AN EXTERNAL RECRUITER

Treat this relationship like any other professional partnership. Here's how to make it work:

- Be clear and detailed.

- Go beyond job descriptions; share your culture, workflow, values, and pain points.

- Designate one point of contact. This keeps communication streamlined and avoids mixed signals.

- Set realistic expectations.

- Be prepared to adjust offers or timelines because strong candidates may take time to surface and secure.

- Respond promptly. Delays in reviewing résumés or scheduling interviews can cost you top talent.

- Invest in the relationship.

- Share feedback, be transparent, and help your recruiter represent you well.

- Ask for their market input. A good recruiter can help you refine offers, job titles, or job ads based on what's resonating in the market.

INTERNAL AND EXTERNAL RECRUITING...IT'S NOT EITHER/OR

You don't have to choose one or the other. Many practices thrive using a hybrid model:

- Use internal resources for technician, CSR, or support staff hiring.

- Bring in external recruiters for DVMs, leadership roles, or expansion needs.

- When internal efforts have stalled, engage a recruiter to act as a force multiplier, not a replacement.

Recruiting is too important to be left to chance. By choosing the right model at the right time and managing that relationship strategically, you'll improve your ability to attract and retain top veterinary talent.

CHECKLIST: CHOOSING THE RIGHT VETERINARY RECRUITER

Use this checklist to evaluate potential recruiting partners:

- They specialize in veterinary recruiting or have extensive animal health experience.

- They understand the specific role(s) you're hiring for.

- They've placed candidates in similar practice types (GP, ER, specialty, nonprofit).

- They provide testimonials or references from other veterinary leaders.

- Their communication style matches your expectations.

- They explain their fee structure clearly (contingency, flat fee, subscription, exclusive).

- They offer candidate guarantees.

- They outline their sourcing and screening strategy.

- They can operate confidentially, if needed.

- They ask questions and invest time in learning your practice culture.

- You trust their professionalism, ethics, and representation of your brand.

QUESTIONS TO ASK A POTENTIAL VETERINARY RECRUITER

Use these questions to assess fit and capability:

- How long have you worked in veterinary recruiting?

- Can you share recent placements in similar roles?

- What's your process for sourcing and screening candidates?

- What's your average time-to-fill for this type of position?

- How will you present our practice to candidates?

- How many similar roles are you recruiting for currently?

- What happens if the candidate doesn't work out?

- Do you offer a replacement guarantee?

- How do you ensure a good cultural fit?

- How do you handle confidentiality for sensitive searches?

- What is your communication cadence and preferred method of contact?

- Can you continue to search on your behalf as well?

Pro Tip: Using an external recruiter should be as comfortable as using any other business professional. Do your homework, and work with those who seem confident, competent, and reputable.

CHAPTER 19

Recruiting Contracts— Read the Fine Print

Read it. Understand it. Keep it handy.

In veterinary recruiting, contracts aren't just legal formalities but essential tools for protecting your practice, clarifying expectations, and building strong, lasting partnerships with recruiters. Understanding what to look for in a recruiting agreement, the roles and responsibilities of both parties, and how to handle potential disputes is critical to avoiding costly surprises.

In this chapter, you'll learn...

- The key clauses every veterinary recruiting agreement should include and why they matter

- How to read the fine print to avoid costly surprises and misunderstandings

- The specific roles and responsibilities of both the hiring practice and the recruiter

- What to do if a recruiting contract is breached and how to protect your practice's interests

WHY CONTRACTS MATTER IN VETERINARY RECRUITING

In veterinary hiring, recruiting contracts are not just paperwork; they are your first defense against misunderstandings, unexpected costs, and damaged relationships. Whether you're a practice owner, manager, or administrator, a well-drafted agreement ensures you know…

- What services you are getting

- What you are paying for and when

- What happens if something goes wrong

Too often, practices and recruiters begin working together on nothing more than a handshake or vague email. That's when problems start and when tens of thousands of dollars in fees, lost productivity, and strained partnerships can be at stake.

A strong recruiting contract will…

- Clarify payment terms and what triggers them.

- Define the scope of services (from candidate sourcing to full-cycle recruitment).

- Establish candidate ownership.

- Outline replacement guarantees or refund policies.

- Specify exclusivity, if applicable.

- Provide legal recourse in the event of a breach.

COMMON TYPES OF VETERINARY RECRUITING AGREEMENTS

While recruiting contracts vary in length and complexity, most fall into three categories.

Category	Description	Contract Should Define...
Contingency Agreements	The recruiter is paid only when you hire a candidate they provide.	• Candidate ownership period • Fee percentage • Guarantee period
Flat-Fee or Subscription Models	A set amount is paid per hire or for a fixed period, regardless of the number of hires.	• Deliverables and scope • Timeframes • Ongoing support provided
Exclusive Agreements	One recruiter or agency has sole authority to fill your role.	These agreements often include more robust service guarantees but require careful review of... • Duration and scope • Cancellation terms

Pro Tip: Always get the agreement in writing, even with a trusted recruiter. A written contract protects both parties if circumstances change.

READING THE FINE PRINT: WHAT TO WATCH FOR

Contracts can appear straightforward but may contain clauses that lead to costly disputes.

Clause	Look closely and consider...
Candidate Ownership Period	How long after submission does a recruiter "own" a candidate? Thirty, sixty, or 180 days can make a big difference.
Backdoor Hire Clauses	What happens if you hire a submitted candidate through another channel or months later?
Payment Terms and Triggers	Is payment due upon offer, start date, or after a probationary period?
Replacement Guarantees	What happens if the candidate leaves early? Free replacement, partial refund, or credit?
Exclusivity Clauses	If exclusive, how long are you bound to one recruiter? Under what conditions can you end exclusivity?
Termination Clauses	How and when can either party end the agreement?

When in doubt, ask for clarification, or better yet, consult an employment law attorney who understands recruiting agreements.

ROLES AND RESPONSIBILITIES: WHO DOES WHAT?

Misunderstandings about responsibilities are among the most common sources of conflict in veterinary recruiting. When both sides fulfill their roles, the relationship becomes a partnership—not just a transaction.

Practice Owners and Hiring Managers Should...	• Clearly define the role, compensation, and desired culture fit
	• Respond promptly to recruiter-submitted candidates
	• Communicate decisions transparently
	• Respect candidate ownership terms and timeframes
Recruiters Should...	• Present qualified, pre-screened candidates
	• Maintain confidentiality and respect candidate preferences
	• Communicate timelines and expectations clearly
	• Accurately represent both the candidate and the clinic

ENFORCING A RECRUITING CONTRACT

Documentation is key. Retain all résumés, submission dates, communications, and interview notes. A thorough paper trail can make or break your case. Most contracts are honored without issue, but follow these steps when a dispute arises, such as a backdoor hire or an unpaid fee.

Start with Communication	Misunderstandings are more common than malice. Discuss the issue directly and document the conversation.
Reference the Agreement	Point to the specific clause and timeline that applies. Keep it factual and professional.
Consider Mediation	If included in the contract, mediation or arbitration can resolve disputes faster and with less expense.
Seek Legal Action (if necessary)	If the amount in dispute is significant, consult an attorney. Ensure your contract specifies governing law and venue for disputes.

FINAL THOUGHTS: PROTECTING THE PARTNERSHIP

Recruiting contracts aren't just about safeguarding fees but preserving trust, professionalism, and clear expectations.

When done right, they form the foundation for long-term recruiting partnerships that help practices grow and professionals thrive. In a field where high-value hires are scarce, clarity, documentation, and mutual respect aren't optional; they're essential.

A good contract won't prevent every problem but will give you a framework to solve them before they become expensive, time-consuming disputes.

Recruiting contracts aren't just about safeguarding fees. They set the foundation for trust, professionalism, and clarity in your hiring relationships. When done right, they help practices attract top talent, reduce misunderstandings, and create partnerships that support long-term growth. A strong contract won't prevent every challenge, but it will give you a framework to address issues efficiently, preserve relationships, and ensure your recruitment efforts are strategic, fair, and effective.

For those considering stepping into full-time recruiting, remember recruitment isn't just about filling roles; it's about shaping the future of veterinary medicine. Clear agreements, defined expectations, and thoughtful partnerships are your first steps toward thriving in this people-driven profession.

CHAPTER 20

So...You Want to Become an External Veterinary Recruiter?

If you love people and matchmaking, this might just be the best job in the world.

Becoming an external veterinary recruiter means stepping into a role that connects veterinary professionals with the proper practices across many locations and specialties. It's a career that requires curiosity, strong communication, and a willingness to learn the nuances of the veterinary industry. It's vital that you understand what the job looks like, who can succeed in it, and how to build a sustainable recruiting business.

In this chapter, you will learn…

- The key differences between internal and external recruiting and why external recruiters play a vital role

- The skills, background, and mindset that make a great veterinary recruiter

- How recruiters typically get paid and the common fee structures you need to know

- Practical steps to build your client base, overcome challenges, and grow your recruiting career

An external veterinary recruiter is a third-party professional who connects veterinary talent (veterinarians, technicians, or leadership) with clinics or organizations that need to hire. The difference between external and internal recruiters is that it is not a single clinic that employs the former. An external recruiter works on behalf of multiple clients in several different niches, such as general practice, ER or ER/specialty, shelters, corporate groups, rural placements, academic positions, leadership roles, and industry.

WHO CAN BE SUCCESSFUL IN THIS ROLE?

You don't need to be a veterinarian, manager, or administrator to be an external recruiter, but you must be willing to learn about the industry in all its wonderful complexity.

Ideal backgrounds:

- Former practice managers and administrators who have experience hiring at the clinical level

- Veterinarians looking for career pivots

- HR professionals with healthcare experience

- Entrepreneurs with strong sales and people skills

Key traits of successful veterinary recruiters:

- Empathetic communicator who builds trust quickly

- Organized and self-motivated, especially when working independently

- Comfortable with rejection and delayed wins

- Curious about understanding the practice culture, market trends, and career goals of candidates

- Service-oriented (This is not about pushing people into jobs; it's about long-term matches.)

WHAT DOES WORK ACTUALLY LOOK LIKE?

Day-to-day breakdown:

- Sourcing candidates via job boards, social media, vet school networks, and referrals

- Conducting initial screens, interviews, and reference checks

- Coordinating interviews and follow-ups with client clinics

- Advising both sides on the offer strategy and negotiation

- Tracking progress and reporting outcomes to clients

You'll need to master...

- Candidate outreach (e.g., cold emails, calls, direct messages, social media)

- Database or customer relationship management (CRM) or applicant tracking system (ATS) basics

- Interview preparation and coaching

- Market compensation knowledge

- Writing compelling job ads and clinic profiles

Pro Tip: Remember that you work for the client, not the candidate, and you have a fiduciary responsibility to your client.

THE TOOLS YOU'LL NEED

Technology stack:

- ATS or CRM

- Social media platforms

- Virtual interviewing platform for video calls

- Phone interview tools, such as a headset, calendar, auto note-taking, and real-time transcription of the interview

- Email automation

- Project management tools

- AI technology

Data management:

- Track contacts, outreach attempts, feedback, and stages

- Create reusable templates and workflows

- Build a personal database of candidates and clinics

HOW YOU GET PAID

When a veterinary practice chooses to work with an external recruiter, the structure of that relationship matters. Different recruiting models come with different expectations, pricing, and levels of involvement. Here are the most common types:

Recruiting Model	How it Works	Payment	Pros	Cons	Best for...
Contingency Search	The recruiter is only paid if and when placement is made.	Typically, a percentage of the hired candidate's first-year salary	Encourages clients to sign up quickly	Can result in more transactional relationships and less focus on long-term fit or strategy	DVM roles, technicians, or when you want to work with multiple recruiters
Retained Search	The recruiter is paid upfront.	Often split into three parts	Focused attention on your role	Higher upfront cost and financial commitment	Executive roles or C-level positions
Subscription Model	Clients pay a monthly flat fee.	Fixed fee regardless of number of placements with typically a month-to-month or quarterly agreement	Predictable costs and budgeting Focus on pipeline building	Requires a longer-term mindset	Clinics with ongoing hiring needs
Flat Fee or Hourly Consulting	You pay a fixed fee or hourly rate for a specific project.		Highly flexible, often budget-friendly, and term needs	Often does not include ongoing candidate sourcing	Startups or new practices setting up a hiring process

CHOOSING THE RIGHT MODEL

Each model serves a different purpose. A contingency search might make sense when you need a DVM fast, but remember most searches today are NOT fast. But if you're building a team, improving retention, or planning for growth, a subscription or consulting-based approach could give you more value over time.

Consider your goals, timeline, and internal capacity, then choose the model that aligns with your broader hiring strategy.

CONTINGENCY FEE STRUCTURE

In a contingency search, the recruiter is paid a percentage of the candidate's first-year salary upon successful placement. This is typically based on the base salary, though some recruiters charge a percentage of the total compensation package, including bonuses or benefits.

For veterinary technicians or support staff, the contingency fee may be structured as a flat rate or a lower percentage of the first-year salary. However, some recruiters caution against significantly reduced percentages, as the effort required to fill these roles can be equally demanding. The overall fee may appear lower simply because support staff salaries are generally lower than those of veterinarians.

Payment is usually due within thirty days of the hire's start date, unless otherwise stated in the contract.

PAYMENT CONSIDERATIONS FOR RECRUITERS

To ensure a smooth and professional payment process, recruiters should…

- Establish clear terms in a signed agreement before beginning the search.

- Define refund or replacement clauses in the event the hire leaves prematurely.

- Include guarantee periods, such as a sixty- or ninety-day window for retention.

- Invoice promptly upon the candidate's start date and track invoice status to avoid delays.

- Setting expectations early and documenting all terms helps protect both parties and builds trust throughout the recruiting process.

HOW TO BUILD YOUR CLIENT BASE

Start with your network, such as former colleagues, clinic owners, and vet school connections. Offer value before asking for business; share a job market update, salary benchmark, or candidate insight.

Tips on marketing yourself:

- Build a strong social media presence and website

- Post valuable content: hiring tips, market trends, spotlight roles

- Join social media groups and professional forums

- Attend CE conferences and career fairs

Keep your reputation golden:

- Never ghost a client or candidate

- Be honest about what's realistic and where you specialize

- Don't post jobs you don't have

- Don't tell clients you have candidates when you don't

- Always aim for a long-term relationship, not a quick deal

CHALLENGES TO EXPECT

Third-party or external recruiters play a vital role in veterinary hiring, but the job comes with unique challenges. Unlike in-house recruiters, external partners must build trust quickly, often without complete visibility into the clinic's culture, workflow, or internal dynamics. They must navigate varying expectations, limited communication access, and competitive timelines, all while representing both the client and the candidate with professionalism. Balancing speed, accuracy, and relationship management is critical—and not always easy.

- Ghosting and drop-offs—yes, even veterinarians do it (both candidates and clients can be guilty)

- Clients who don't follow through, such as delaying interviews, not providing feedback, and so on

- Long sales cycles, with some roles taking months to fill

- You work on spec, which means you are working and only getting paid if it leads to a placement, unless retained; be selective with who you invest in

- Market volatility—clinic needs shift, graduates relocate, and techs burn out

REWARDS AND IMPACT

While external recruiters often work under pressure and without guaranteed pay, the role offers unique rewards. Third-party recruiters have the power to shape careers, support clinics in critical hiring moments, and build lasting relationships across the industry. The work is fast-paced, challenging, entrepreneurial, and deeply rewarding for those who thrive on connection and results.

Becoming an external veterinary recruiter isn't easy, but it's incredibly impactful to clients and candidates and a rewarding career where you're helping both people and practices thrive. Moreover, it's financially satisfying; successful recruiters can earn six to seven figures with consistency. You have schedule freedom, which is excellent for those who value remote work and autonomy. Plus, you can gain industry respect because great recruiters are remembered and referred. Finally, there is an emotional payoff as you're helping veterinarians and other top talent find better jobs and clinics build better teams.

Without question, you'll need resilience, strategy, and a heart for people. But if you're willing to build relationships over transactions, you can become a trusted voice in an amazing industry.

About the Author

Gwendolyn Lowder Delavar, CPVR, is a trailblazer in veterinary recruiting with more than three decades of experience helping practices across the United States and beyond build strong, effective teams. She launched her recruiting career in 1992, starting from scratch with nothing more than a landline phone, the Yellow Pages, and an unwavering determination to serve the veterinary community. In 2024, she founded the National Veterinary Talent Acquisition Association™ (NVTAA™), the first organization of its kind dedicated to advancing recruiting practices within the veterinary industry.

As founder and president of VetProCentral™, Gwendolyn has worked with thousands of practice owners and managers, providing both recruiting expertise and business insights that have shaped the way veterinary practices hire, train, and retain talent. Known for her professionalism, persistence, and passion for elevating veterinary medicine through people, she has become a trusted partner and mentor to recruiters, managers, and veterinarians alike.

Today, she leads a dedicated team of recruiters and specialists based in San Diego, serving clients throughout the U.S., Canada, and Hong Kong. When she isn't matching top talent with thriving practices, Gwendolyn enjoys spending time with her family, friends, and, of course, her dogs! Gwendolyn loves hearing from anyone within the industry who would like to chat about the book, veterinary recruiting, or the veterinary world in general!

CONNECT WITH GWENDOLYN LOWDER DELAVAR

- Website: www.vetprocentral.com
- Email: gwen@vetprocentral.com
- LinkedIn: https://www.linkedin.com/in/gwendelavar/

For speaking, consulting, or recruiting support, visit www.vetprocentral.com.

www.ingramcontent.com/pod-product-compliance
Lightning Source LLC
Chambersburg PA
CBHW030518210326
41597CB00013B/954